BEST OF

Brussels

Paul Smitz

Best of Brussels
1st edition – March 2004
Published by Lonely Planet Publications Pty Ltd
ABN 36 005 607 983

Australia Head Office, Locked Bag 1, Footscray, Vic 3011
☎ 03 8379 8000 fax 03 8379 8111
talk2us@lonelyplanet.com.au
USA 150 Linden St, Oakland, CA 94607
☎ 510 893 8555 toll free 800 275 8555
fax 510 893 8572
info@lonelyplanet.com
UK 72–82 Rosebery Avenue, London EC1R 4RW
☎ 020 7841 9000 fax 020 7841 9001
go@lonelyplanet.co.uk
France 1 rue du Dahomey, 75011 Paris
☎ 01 55 25 33 00 fax 01 55 25 33 01
bip@lonelyplanet.fr
www.lonelyplanet.fr

This title was commissioned in Lonely Planet's London office and produced by: **Commissioning Editors** Sam Trafford & Judith Bamber **Coordinating Editor** Stephanie Pearson **Coordinating Cartographer** Kusnandar **Layout Designer** Cris Gibcus **Proofer** Helen Yeates **Indexer** Stephanie Pearson **Cartographers** Jarrad Needham, Sarah Sloane, Chris Tsismetzis **Managing Cartographer** Mark Griffiths **Cover Designer** Wendy Wright **Project Manager** Charles Rawlings-Way **Series Designer** Gerilyn Attebery **Mapping Development** Paul Piaia **Regional Publishing Manager** Katrina Browning **Thanks to** Adriana Mammarella, Diana Saad, Kalya Ryan, Lachlan Ross, LPI, Martin Heng, Michelle Lewis, Nic Lehman

Photographs by Lonely Planet Images and Jean-Bernard Carillet except for the following as listed: p5, p36, p79 Martin Moos/Lonely Planet Images; p13 Tamsin Wilson/ Lonely Planet Images. **Cover photograph** Grand Place with Christmas lighting in Brussels, Belgium, Colour Day Production/Getty Images. All images are copyright of the photographers unless otherwise indicated. Many of the images in this guide are available for licensing from Lonely Planet Images: www.lonelyplanetimages.com.

ISBN 1 74059 388 X

Printed through Colorcraft Ltd, Hong Kong
Printed in China

Acknowledgements © Brussels Transit Map STIB/MIVB 2004

HOW TO USE THIS BOOK

Colour-Coding & Maps

Each chapter has a colour code along the banner at the top of the page, which is also used for text and symbols on maps (eg all venues reviewed in the Highlights chapter are orange on the maps). The fold-out maps inside the front and back covers are numbered from 1 to 4. All sights and venues in the text have map references; eg (2, D5) means Map 2, grid reference D5. See p96 for map symbols.

Prices

Concession prices can include senior, student, member or coupon discounts. Meal cost and room rate categories are listed at the start of the Eating and Sleeping chapters, respectively.

Text Symbols

- ☎ telephone
- ✉ address
- email/website address
- € admission
- opening hours
- i information
- M metro
- tram
- bus
- wheelchair access
- on-site/nearby eatery
- child-friendly venue
- V good vegetarian selection
- smoke-free venue

Contents

From the Publisher

AUTHOR

Paul Smitz

Paul was well qualified to work through the best of what Brussels has to offer (scattering empty plates, glasses and badly pronounced French *mots* in his wake) due to his lengthy Belgian lineage, a local group of enthusiastic relatives and an impressive dedication to the art of self-satisfaction. He thoroughly enjoyed re-experiencing a city often pigeonholed by its political connections, but which in reality has a depth of urban character and a simple appreciation of life that's hard to beat. He has learned many things about Brussels, including the fact that Audrey Hepburn was born here and that you probably shouldn't eat snail soup before testing out the next generation of amusement-park rides. He also apologises for the joke about Jean-Claude Van Damme and the 'mussels from Brussels'.

For their help and all-round warmth, Paul would like to give heartfelt thanks to Suzanne and Daniel, Séverine and Marc, Sophie and François, and Tass and Cris. Thanks also go to Leanne Logan and Geert Cole for giving him heaps of great ideas to plagiarise, and to his LP co-workers on this project. Most of all, thanks to Katie for all the help, the company and for leaving Melanie Safka at home.

PHOTOGRAPHER

Jean-Bernard Carillet

A Paris-based author and photographer, Jean-Bernard has contributed to numerous LP guides, in French and in English. When not shooting some crystal-clear lagoons in the tropics or markets in eastern Africa, he goes regularly to eastern France, southern Belgium and the Ruhr in Germany to work on a darker subject – the remaining industrial wasteland.

SEND US YOUR FEEDBACK

We love to hear from travellers – your comments keep us on our toes and help make our books better. Our well-travelled team reads every word on what you loved or loathed about this book. Although we cannot reply individually to postal submissions, we always guarantee that your feedback goes straight to the appropriate authors, in time for the next edition – and the most useful submissions are rewarded with a free book. To send us your updates – and find out about LP events, newsletters and travel news – visit our award-winning website www.lonelyplanet.com.

Note: We may edit, reproduce and incorporate your comments in Lonely Planet products such as guidebooks, websites and digital products, so let us know if you don't want your comments reproduced or your name acknowledged. For a copy of our privacy policy visit www.lonelyplanet.com/privacy.

Lonely Planet books provide independent advice. Lonely Planet does not accept advertising in guidebooks, nor do we accept payment in exchange for listing or endorsing any place or business. Lonely Planet writers do not accept discounts or payments in exchange for positive coverage of any sort.

Introducing Brussels

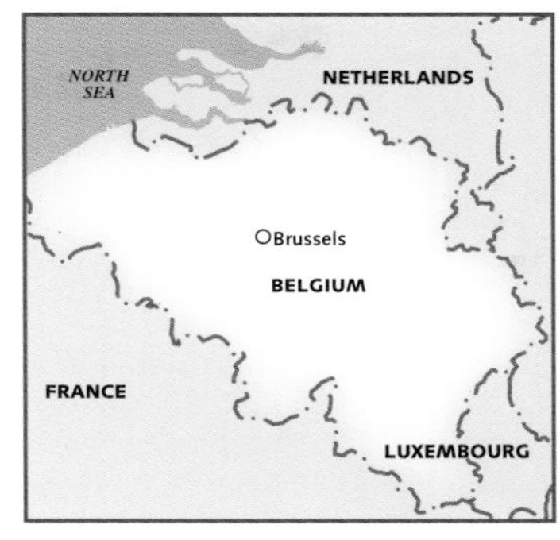

Brussels (Bruxelles in French, Brussel in Flemish) is the real urban deal, a refreshingly down-to-earth yet vivacious cosmopolitan habitat decorated with sublime Art Nouveau–lined streets, fashionable shop fronts, beer-washed old-world pubs, soaring palaces, jazzed-up clubs, inspired artworks, restaurant tables piled high with plates of superlative multicultural food, and chocolate-coated smiles.

The aptly named capital of Europe reveals itself in memorable vignettes: apartment facades splashed with the red of windowboxed *roi du balcon* ('king of the balcony', also known as geraniums); throngs of people ebbing and flowing down the fabulous cobblestoned *rues* (streets) of the medieval centre; the moon glowing above the baroque peaks of Grand Place; craggy old Bruxellois playing chess among foaming glasses; people scanning newspapers in wonderful formal gardens with a pantheon of bronze statues reading over their shoulders; a Magritte landscape pulling you into its surreal depths; Eurocrats talking policies through mouthfuls of mussels; tray-balanced cocktails veering over the heads of a chattering crowd in a table-packed square...

In between tracing the patterns of exquisite lace-work and stroking the cat stretched out next to you in the leather-padded booth of a grand café, let the high-spirited and genuinely friendly locals teach you something about appreciating life – follow their lead in lingering over every mouthful of a slow lunch, having a sociable haggle in a communal flea market and shrugging off your cares to have a good long laugh. Brussels is a city to savour, so sit back and just breathe it all in.

MARTIN MOOS

Grand Place (p8) lives up to its name at night

Neighbourhoods

The Belgian capital is surrounded by a thrumming motorway known as the Ring, while angling around the old city centre is a pentagon of busy boulevards called the Petit (Small) Ring. Central Brussels is divided into two main areas: the Lower Town and the Upper Town.

Off the Beaten Track

To get away from maddening crowds, evacuate yourself to:

- the greenery of Forêt de Soignes (p27)
- the uncrowded terraces of Le Botanique (p28)
- the meditative Église Sts Pierre et Guidon (p27)
- the Art Nouveau backstreets of St Gilles and Ixelles (p33)
- Jardin Botanique National's expansive grounds (p37)

Escape to Jardin Botanique National

The **Lower Town** is Brussels' compact medieval core, threaded by cobblestoned streets and with the stunning Grand Place as its ancient centrepiece. Northwest of Grand Place is a tiny, enigmatic quarter called **Ilôt Sacré**, which is filled with traditional restaurants, while to the west, just beyond the landmark Bourse (stock exchange), are the sublime districts of **St Géry** and **Ste Catherine**. St Géry is full of designer bars and designer people, while Ste Catherine prefers good old-fashioned serenity to full-frontal trendiness. In the Lower Town's southwest is the **Marolles**, the city's working-class heartland, where you'll still hear locals speaking Bruxellois, an old dialect based on a mixture of Flemish and French.

The **Upper Town** is the old aristocratic quarter, as evidenced by its wide boulevards and weighty buildings, and is scattered across the heights to the east and southeast of Grand Place. Many of the city's finest museums choose to hang out near the central Place Royale, as do the Palais Royal (Royal Palace) and various embassies. To the southwest of Place Royale is the **Sablon**, where modern-day aristocrats buy antiques and then browse fashion boutiques on nearby Avenue Louise.

East of the centre is the **EU area**, dominated by the mighty European Parliament and other Eurocrat high-rises, while straddling Avenue Louise to the south is the affluent commune of **Ixelles**, which along with neighbouring **St Gilles** has famous Art Nouveau architecture. In the north of Ixelles, around Porte de Namur, is the **Matongé** district, where Brussels' African community conducts its business. North of the centre are the immigrant neighbourhoods of **St Josse** and **Schaerbeek**, and beyond them is leafy **Laeken**, whose main tenant is the Belgian royal estate. West and southwest of the centre are the peaceful suburbs of **Molenbeek-St-Jean** and **Anderlecht**.

Itineraries

Brussels not only has a wealth of outstanding museums, picturesque galleries, sculpted gardens and beautiful Art Nouveau architecture, but is also laced with refreshing greenery and urbane, ego-burnishing haunts. If you have only a day or three to make the pleasure of Brussels' acquaintance, try the following suggestions.

DAY ONE

Run your eyes around Grand Place's magnificent skyline before burrowing through waiters in Rue des Bouchers to inspect the Galeries St Hubert glasshouse. Scale the Upper Town to snoop around the Musées Royaux des Beaux-Arts de Belgique and the Musée des Instruments de Musique. Stroll through Parc de Bruxelles before scoffing chocolates in the Sablon and heading to St Géry for a gregarious nightcap.

DAY TWO

Sift trash and treasure at the Marolles flea market, then ride the elevator to Place Poelaert and admire the view before letting the Palais de Justice overwhelm you. Fill shopping bags on Avenue Louise, then roam Ixelles' Art Nouveau streets to arrive at the extraordinary Musée Horta. Taste an authentic Belgian brew at the Musée Bruxellois de la Gueuze before raising a glass in an old Brussels pub and filling up on seafood in Ste Catherine.

DAY THREE

Browse comic art in the Centre Belge de la Bande Dessinée, then head to Parc de Cinquantenaire to admire its arcade and museums. Get political at the European Parliament before sampling the vibrant atmosphere of Matongé. Spend the evening reclining under a grand café's chandelier or licking your plate clean in a modern restaurant, then wander the Lower Town's spot-lit cobblestones.

Worst of Brussels

- rip-off restaurants around Grand Place
- fearing for your life on pedestrian crossings
- some unbelievably ugly contemporary architecture
- ashen skies
- wiping a dog turd off your shoe (again)

The bright lights of Rue des Bouchers

Highlights

GRAND PLACE (2, D5)

The first time you emerge into this enormous, open-air square, surrounded by gorgeous facades and crisscrossed by excitable visitors, you'll understand why it's called Grand Place. Cynics will say that the name is also a reference to the size of the bill you'll encounter in the many overpriced eateries in its vicinity, but this is merely in keeping with the square's history as Brussels' commercial centre. Try not to get too fazed by the inevitable crowds and find yourself a spare chunk of paving from where you can take in the dazzling baroque and Gothic horizon formed by the tops of the buildings.

INFORMATION

- ✉ Grand Place, Lower Town
- Ⓜ De Brouckère
- Bourse premetro
- ♿ fair
- ✕ Le Roy d'Espagne (p50)

The Gothic facade of Hôtel de Ville

The site was a clump of marshland until the first cobblestones were arranged here in the 12th century. It was initially used as a large marketplace under the name Grote Markt, which by the 14th century had leaked into the surrounding thoroughfares. This explains the commerce-oriented names of the adjoining streets such as Rue des Bouchers (Butchers Street), Rue du Marché aux Fromages (Cheese Market Street) and, continuing the dairy theme, Rue au Beurre (Butter Street). The prosperity of Brussels at that time was further emphasised by the erection (from 1401 to 1459) of the monumentally Gothic **Hôtel de Ville** (p25), still used today as the city's town hall, and several dozen beautifully adorned merchant **guildhalls** (see the boxed text on p75).

The majority of the guildhalls standing today date from the end of the 17th century (see the boxed text opposite). Following are some of the highlights of this historic grouping, all worth a close inspection. The **Maison des Boulangers** (Bakers' House; No 1) once belonged to the bakers' guild, as evidenced by the bust of their patron St Albert over the front door, but today hosts the busy café Le Roy d'Espagne (p50). **Le Cornet** (The Horn; No 6) is identifiable as the home of the boatmen's guild by its stern-shaped gable, while next door is **Le Renard** (The Fox), which housed the haberdashers' guild and is topped by a statue of St Nicolas, patron saint of merchants. **L'Étoile** (The Star; No 8) is the smallest house on the square and was where guild advocate Everard 't Serclaes was murdered in 1388 by cronies of the Count of Flanders, an event commemorated by a statue (p31) in the arcade below. **Le Cygne** (The Swan; No 9) hosted the butchers' guild and later a workers' café that counted Karl Marx among its pat rons. **Le Pigeon** (Nos 26 and 27) belonged to the artists' guild and in 1852 famously let a room to Victor Hugo.

The building lined with busts whose gilded exterior dominates the square's southeastern end is called **Le Maison des Ducs de Brabant** (The House of the Dukes of Brabant) and comprises half a dozen neoclassical guildhalls. Another prominent building is the **Maison du Roi** (King's House), which apparently once housed Spanish royalty and now sets the scene for the outstanding Musée de la Ville de Bruxelles (p22).

The centre of Grand Place is regularly transformed into a stony stage for various events, from floral carpets and mock jousting events to night-time summer concerts, when half the city seems jammed into the square. It's also where people rendezvous in the late afternoon to plan the evening's activities, or just sit at a café and bemusedly watch tourists filming tourists filming the architecture.

Quick-fire Renovations

On 13 August 1695, France's territory-hungry Louis XIV began a 36-hour cannonball bombardment of Grand Place from beyond the city walls, severely damaging or destroying every building bar the Hôtel de Ville and two guildhalls. The indefatigable Bruxellois entirely rebuilt the square in superb Flemish Renaissance style within four years.

A reminder of the renovations

Follow the herd to see Brussels' 17th-century guidhalls

BEER

There's no shortage of beer merchants

Beer *(bière)* is not just a drink in Belgium – it's a food group. The country produces a staggering array of somewhere between 500 and 600 brews, though some estimates range as high as 800. Obviously not all of these beers are deserving of a gold medal and the declaration of a national holiday in their honour, particularly some of the bigger-means-blander drinks mass-produced by global brewing conglomerates. But the sheer diversity and overall quality of Belgium's beer production is second to none. Even if beer isn't a personal favourite, try being a prospector for liquid gold during your stay in Brussels. Educate your palate in the range of exquisite tastes, drink up the atmosphere in the delightful old cafés, and charge your glass in the company of the relaxed Bruxellois. To do otherwise is to miss out on an intrinsic part of this city's beer-loving culture.

The credit for Belgium's oversupply of beer is allegedly due to St Arnold, patron saint of brewers, who in the Middle Ages came up with a fantastic rationale for having a quaff: it prevented the plague. His reasoning was that as the plague was being contracted through the drinking of unboiled water, people should instead drink beer (which is subjected to boiling). Dismissing the alternative solution of just boiling their drinking water, people adopted this miracle cure with gusto and set a precedent that continues to this day. At the beginning of the 20th century, Belgium had more than 3000 working breweries. By early 2003, after decades of natural attrition, market pressures and the engulfing of family-owned businesses by export-hungry multinationals, the number had dwindled to around 115.

Mappa Mundo, one of many city bars

One of the frustrations of visiting Brussels is that there are so many styles of beer to sample and so little time to sample them. But the important thing to remember with Belgian beer is that it's designed to be tasted, not guzzled. If you gulp lots of different beers in rapid succession, you'll minimise your appreciation of individual flavours (not to mention your appreciation of life the morning after).

DON'T MISS

- drinking in a classic old brown café or among Art Nouveau grandeur (p61)
- tasting a Westmalle Tripel, Duvel and Cantillon Gueuze
- breathing in the history of the Cantillon brewery (p14)
- ordering Kwak and receiving a potion flask in a wooden stand
- buying the *Good Beer Guide to Belgium & Holland* by Tim Webb

To confirm that beer is indeed a religion in this country, six of its Trappist monasteries are officially allowed to produce and market beers using the 'Trappist' trademark. Their products – Achel, Chimay, Orval, Rochefort, Westmalle and Westvleteren beers – are characterised by a gold or dark colour, a smooth taste and a lofty alcohol content of between 6% and 11.3%. White beers (*bière blanche* in French or *witbier* in Flemish), meanwhile, are pale and cloudy wheat beers that have a relatively low alcohol content (4% to 5.5%) but a high refreshment factor, which explains why there's a big demand for them internationally. One of the main white-beer brands is Hoegaarden.

The country's most revered beer is the unique *lambic* (*lambiek* in Flemish), a liquid that is spontaneously fermented and stored in barrels for up to three years before being deemed drinkable. The different types of *lambic* include fruit versions such as *kriek* (made with cherries) and *framboise* (made with raspberries), but the queen brew is the dry, slightly bitter *gueuze* – stick to traditional *gueuze* brewers like Cantillon and Girardin, and avoid commercial efforts like Mort Subite or St Louis. Other broad styles include Abbey beers, which without exception involve abbeys licensing their names to brewing concerns to get a share of the genuine Trappist market; full-strength brown ales like Kapittel Prior and Gauloise Brune, though these are a disappearing breed; full-bodied golden or blonde ales like the delicious Duvel; and seasonal beers, particularly the rich, dark brews that emerge over winter.

So many beers, so little time

CATHÉDRALE DES STS MICHEL & GUDULE (1, E3)

The construction of Belgium's massive, stately national church, with its double-towered facade and conspicuous slate-grey central turret, began around 1226 and was finally finished some 300 years later. However, the church continued to suffer a reputation as a 'renovator's dream' and endured many later refinements, including a recent 16-year-long touch-up. The church is dedicated to Brussels' male and female patron saints (Michel and Gudule, respectively) and is considered to be the country's most outstanding example of Brabant Gothic architecture. A major event here was the marriage in April 2003 of future monarch Prince Laurent and princess-to-be Claire Coombs.

INFORMATION

- ☎ 02 217 83 45
- www.cathedralestmichel.be
- ✉ Parvis Ste Gudule, Upper Town
- € treasury €1; Romanesque ruins €1 donation
- treasury 10am-12.30pm & 2-5pm
- ⓘ organ concerts usually held 8pm Tue
- Ⓜ Gare Centrale
- fair
- Aux Armes de Bruxelles (p49)

The interior is sparsely decorated because it was plundered by Protestants in the late 16th century and again 200 years later by the French army, and obviously lacked a dependable new-for-old insurance policy. However, one piece of grand ornamentation is the baroque pulpit, carved by Henri-François Verbruggen in 1699 and depicting Adam's and Eve's hurried exit from Eden. A walk down the nave takes you through a gauntlet of intimidating statuary.

Colour is provided by the church's splendid stained-glass windows, including several by Jean Haeck and the beautiful Renaissance Last Judgment window over the front doors. Just before the transept, gaze up at the enormous new 4300-pipe organ, which seems suspended in midair. It's also possible to see the ruins of an 11th-century **Romanesque church**, built to replace a chapel dedicated to St Michel in the 9th century, and to browse the impressive **treasury** in the flamboyant Blessed Sacrament of the Miracle chapel.

DON'T MISS

- the elaborate oak confessional
- the glittering Monstrance of the Blessed Sacrament in the treasury
- the gilded-copper High Altar
- attending an organ concert

The ornately carved baroque pulpit

CENTRE BELGE DE LA BANDE DESSINÉE (1, E3)

The Belgian Centre for Comic Strip Art is a grand, ambitious showcase of the illustrated stories that have been humouring, confounding and inspiring local and foreign enthusiasts for decades. The impact of this extensive collection of works by the nation's favourite comic artists is heightened by its setting, the stupendous Grand Magasin Waucquez, an Art Nouveau department store created in 1906 by Victor Horta and meticulously restored before being reborn as a museum.

The upstairs galleries, accessed via a lovely sky-lit entrance hall embellished with a Tintin statue, reveal the origins of Belgian comic-strip art, from the publication of *Tintin au Pays des Soviets* (Tintin in the Land of the Soviets) by Hergé in 1929, to the post-WWII creation of *Suske en Wiske* (Bob and Bobette) by Willy Vandersteen and Morris' cowboy parody *Lucky Luke*. Also appearing around this time were the little blue guys and gals that creator Peyo (aka Pierre Culliford) called *Le Schtroumpf*, but who were known in English as the Smurfs.

The museum's top level is devoted to modern strips from the 1960s onwards, and contains the work of many relative newcomers to the craft, including social satire and exhilarating sci-fi and fantasy concepts. Part of the exhibition explains how comic strips are assembled, from preliminary sketches to fully coloured artwork, and there are life-size comic scenes for kids to play character actor in. Serious strip connoisseurs may want to utilise the library and documentation centre.

INFORMATION

- ☎ 02 219 19 80
- www.brusselsbdtour.com/cbbd.htm (French only)
- ✉ Rue des Sables 20, Lower Town
- € adult/child €6.25/2.50
- 10am-6pm Tue-Sun
- i free English-language folder available at reception
- M Gare Centrale
- ♿ good
- ✕ Brasserie Horta (on site)

TAMSIN WILSON

Tintin meets Horta in the entrance hall

Les Cités Obscures

To sample the profoundly inventive ideas flourishing in Belgium's comic-art industry, read *Les Cités Obscures* (www.urbicande.be) by artist François Schuiten and author Benoît Peeters. This fantastical multivolume saga of strange parallel-universe cities includes the story *Brüsel*, a parable whose real-life theme is the EU's recent domination of Brussels.

MUSÉE BRUXELLOIS DE LA GUEUZE (1, A5)

A wander through the dark, musty interior of the superb old Cantillon Brewery, with its narrow wooden ladders, cramped lofts and barrel-crammed cellar, is not just an exercise in understanding how this modest outfit goes about producing some of the finest beer in Belgium. It also exposes you to a traditional Bruxellois enterprise that has taken up the working lives of three generations of one family.

INFORMATION

- ☎ 02 521 49 28
- www.cantillon.be
- ✉ Rue Gheude 56, Anderlecht
- € €3.50
- 9am-5pm Mon-Fri, 10am-5pm Sat
- (i) guided visits by reservation
- (M) Gare du Midi
- L'Étoile d'Or (p54)

The brewery was established by Paul Cantillon in 1900, when it competed with hundreds of other beer factories in Brussels. It's now one of the few remaining Belgian breweries that relies solely on spontaneous fermentation to make its *lambic*, which is then used to create the venerable *gueuze*, plus *kriek* and other fruit beers. Working your way through the atmospheric rooms, you learn how crushed cereals are mixed with warm water in a mashing tun to eventually produce wort. Aged hops are then added as flavouring to the wort, which is cooked, cooled, and the hops filtered out. The liquid is then attic-stored in an impressive copper tun, where wild airborne yeasts enter the fray – it's these yeasts that react with sugars in the wort when it's stored in oak or chestnut barrels that prompt spontaneous fermentation.

The fermentation process for traditional *lambic* can take up to three years, but some modern brewers concoct their own low-brow *lambic* within several weeks and conveniently forget to explain the qualitative difference to consumers. Naturally, the tour finishes with a tasting.

An Explosive Taste

One of Cantillon's exceptional brews is *faro*, a sweet mixture of *lambic*, caramel and candy sugar. But if you buy it, drink it within a month. Otherwise, in the manufacturer's wise words, 'the addition of sugar causes such strong fermentation that the bottles might explode as a result of CO_2 pressure'.

Good beer takes time – up to three years, in fact

MUSÉE DAVID ET ALICE VAN BUUREN

The sublime Museum of David and Alice van Buuren, situated in Brussels' genteel southern suburbs, is three exhibits in one: a classic Art Deco house brimming with original fittings, its outstanding collection of 15th- to 20th-century art, and a magnificent 1.5-hectare garden out back to complete the set. In the 1920s, Dutch banker David van Buuren and his wife, Belgian Alice Piette, began kitting the house out with its then-contemporary furniture, carpets, light fittings and other marvellous domestic decorations of the era, simultaneously honing their socialite skills by courting a stream of VIPs, many well-known artists among them.

A keen and eclectic art connoisseur, van Buuren began acquiring paintings in 1913 and added to the collection up until his death in 1955, with a five-year interruption during WWII when the Jewish couple fled into temporary exile in the US. At the heart of the collection are old Flemish and Italian masters like James Ensor and Francesco Guardi, along with modern Belgian paintings by the likes of Rik Wouters. The standout piece is arguably the wood-painted copy of *Fall of Icarus* by Pieter Breugel the Elder, a canvas version of which currently resides in the Musées Royaux des Beaux-Arts de Belgique (p18). Another exemplary item is the Van Gogh charcoal-and-watercolour sketch *The Potato Peeler*, believed to be the precursor to *The Potato Eaters*.

INFORMATION

- ☎ 02 343 48 51
- www.museumvanbuuren.com
- ✉ Ave Léo Errera 41, Uccle
- € museum & garden adult/child under 10/student €10/free/5; garden only €5/free/2.50
- museum 1-6pm Mon & Sun, 2-6pm Wed; garden 2-5.30pm daily
- ⓘ biennial sculpture exhibitions held in the garden
- No 23 or 90 to Rond-Point Winston Churchill
- La Quincaillerie (p51)

Domestic Art Deco

The **garden** was extensively reworked in the late 1960s to incorporate a yew-tree labyrinth, courtesy of landscape designer René Pechère. It also harbours a number of bronze sculptures.

DON'T MISS

- *Woman Thinking* by Kees van Dongen
- swooning in the romantic 'Garden of the Heart'
- exploring every aspect of the fabulous Art Deco dining room
- Paul Signac's vibrant watercolour *Vase of Flowers*

MUSÉE HORTA

(Map p33)

It's fitting that the Horta Museum is situated in St Gilles, as this commune and neighbouring Ixelles are regarded as the cradle of Belgian Art Nouveau, the fluid and sinuous architectural style pioneered in Brussels by Victor Horta in the 1890s. Horta unveiled his first Art Nouveau effort, the Hôtel Tassel (p33), in 1893, followed by such masterpieces as the Hôtel Solvay (p33), the Maison du Peuple (former headquarters of the Socialist Party, sadly torn down by bureaucrats in 1965) and the Grand Magasin Waucquez (now the Centre Belge de la Bande Dessinée; p13). Between 1898 and 1901 he also built his own home and adjoining studio on Rue Américaine, where he lived and worked for 20 years and which is now one of Brussels' most popular museums.

Horta's breathtaking designs weren't just applied to a building's exterior but to everything inside it, from the furniture and wallpaper to banisters, lights and doorknobs, a philosophy beautifully memorialised in his former home. Take your sweet time as you walk around the various levels of the house and let your eyes settle on the aesthetic minutiae: the way natural light roams around the building; the white enamelled brickwork of the dining room; the banister fusing with the armrest of the couch in the music room; the knotted doorknobs, ornate door hinges, arabesque ironwork, stained glass...

In the cellar are fragments of deconstructed Art Nouveau stonework, as well as a model of the Maison du Peuple.

INFORMATION

- ☎ 02 543 04 90
- www.hortamuseum.be
- Rue Américaine 25, St Gilles
- € adult/child/concession €5/2.50/3.70
- 2-5.30pm Tue-Sun
- ℹ full-colour museum guidebook €11
- Horta premetro; No 91 or 92 from Place Louise
- Le Khnopff (p52)

Shedding some light on Art Nouveau

DON'T MISS

- melted light fixtures in the music room
- gazing down the main stairwell from the top level
- the 2nd-floor winter garden
- discovering the cupboard urinal in the 1st-floor bedroom

MUSÉE ROYAL DE L'AFRIQUE CENTRALE (4, C3)

The Royal Museum for Central Africa is a controversial inclusion in a list of Brussels' highlights. From its inception as Musée du Congo in 1898 to the current identity adopted after Zaire's (now the Democratic Republic of Congo) independence in 1959, it has been a colonial showpiece for Belgian conduct in central Africa, promoting the supposedly idealistic nature of the euphemistic Congo Free State founded by Léopold II in 1885. In reality the tyrannical Léopold II spent two decades plundering the region of ivory and rubber, generating more wealth through slavery, and using the proceeds to fund egomaniacal building projects in Brussels.

So why visit? Because Belgium is reluctantly acknowledging that terrible things happened in the Congo and this has prompted the museum to refocus on central African societies and environments. The fascinating zoological collection has everything from elephants and okapis to foot-long stick insects, while the ethnographic section displays an incredible array of indigenous sculptures, musical instruments, masks, a huge pirogue (dugout canoe) and other artefacts you simply won't see elsewhere outside Africa. There are also great temporary exhibitions of Congolese art, which have included the works of uncompromising realist Chéri Samba, and an enormous park.

There's no doubt the museum still suffers from Congo denial, maintaining a less-than-critical perspective on Léopold II's 'vision' and its fatal consequences. But public interest and opinion are powerful initiators of change, so visit the museum, ask lots of questions and read between the lines.

INFORMATION

- ☎ 02 769 52 11
- www.africamuseum.be
- ✉ Leuvensesteenweg 13, Tervuren
- € adult/child/concession/senior €4/free/1.50/3
- 10am-5pm Tue-Fri, 10am-6pm Sat & Sun
- i most labels are in French and Flemish, but more English is gradually being added
- M Montgomery, then tram No 44 to Tervuren terminus, then exit terminus and walk 300m alongside main road
- ♿ excellent
- ✕ Simba Café (on site)

Out of Africa: items from the museum

An Informed View

For an excellent, critically acclaimed exposition of Léopold II's land-grab in central Africa and how he sold the idea to the world (without revealing his true motives) with the enthusiastic help of luminaries such as explorer Henry Stanley, read the disturbing *King Leopold's Ghost* by Adam Hochschild.

MUSÉES ROYAUX DES BEAUX-ARTS DE BELGIQUE (1, D4)

The Royal Museums of Fine Arts of Belgium is blessed with a priceless collection of artworks from the 14th century right up to the third millennium. It's technically composed of two separate museums, both accessed via a spacious entry hall: the **Museum of Ancient Art**, founded in 1801 and displaying paintings and sculpture up to the 19th century; and the **Museum of Modern Art**, which opened in 1984 and is obsessed with the 20th century. If you think you can check out this museum between lunch and a late-afternoon Brugs Blond, think again – you'll need a full day to even begin to appreciate the creative brilliance on show here.

Clutching your free colour-coded map, start with the ancient art. Works from the 15th and 16th centuries (blue route) include pieces by Hans Memling and Hieronymus Bosch, whose mutant *Triptyque de la Tentation de Saint Antoine* is a highlight, followed by Breugel the Elder's bleak *Les Massacre des Innocents*. The 17th- and 18th-century collection (brown route) is dominated by two roomfuls of Rubens, including the overwhelming *Adoration of the Magi*. The modern art section kicks off with 19th-century pieces (yellow route), comprising Meunier social art, Delacroix neoclassicism and Signac seascapes. Finally you reach the 20th century (green route), where the Flemish expressionism of Permeke hangs out with the entertainingly surreal Magritte, the unpredictable Delvaux and the incomprehensible abstraction of the 'Zero Group'.

The museum also stages major retrospectives, with Belgian symbolist spearhead Fernand Khnopff getting his turn early in 2004.

INFORMATION

- ☎ 02 508 32 11
- www.fine-arts-museum.be
- ✉ Rue de la Régence 3, Upper Town
- € adult/child/student €5/2/3.50; audio guides €2.50
- 10am-5pm Tue-Sun
- ⓘ certain sections close for one hour daily
- Ⓜ Parc
- excellent
- on-site cafeteria

Old meets new, both inside and out

DON'T MISS

- Paul Delvaux's eerie *L'Incendie*
- the sculpture garden beside the main entrance
- *Des Caresses* by Fernand Khnopff
- *Vue de Bruxelles*, Jon Baptist Bonnecroy's intricate rendering of 17th-century Brussels

PARC DU CINQUANTENAIRE (3, C2)

The huge block of greenery and gravel in the eastern half of the EU area, traversed by a row of spectacular arches winged with enormous buildings, is the Parc du Cinquantenaire. It was Léopold II's glorious signature project for Brussels, dreamed up while he was suffering from a severe case of Paris-envy to mark the first 50 years of the Belgian state in 1880. The Parisian overtones are obvious in the Charles Girault-designed **Arcade du Cinquantenaire** (p24), a wannabe Arc de Triomphe that, unfortunately for the Golden Jubilee it was supposed to celebrate, wasn't finished until nearly 25 years after the event.

INFORMATION

- ✉ Parc du Cinquantenaire, EU Area
- 🕓 8am-6pm Oct–mid-Apr, 8am-7pm mid-Apr–end Apr, 8am-9pm May-Sep
- Ⓜ Mérode
- ♿ good
- ✕ Balthazar (p48)

Beyond the semicircular colonnades sandwiching the triumphal arch are the grand halls that housed the Cinquantenaire's official exhibition, now occupied by diverse museums. The southern wing of what's collectively called the Palais du Cinquantenaire houses the **Musée du Cinquantenaire** (p23) and its treasure-trove of decorative arts, as well as **Autoworld**, the adult version of a matchbox-car museum. The northern wing contains the **Musée Royale de l'Armée et d'Histoire Militaire** and its bewildering collection of combative artefacts. Nearby is **Maison Cauchie** (3, D3; ☎ 02 673 15 06; Rue des Francs 5; admission €4; 🕓 11am-1pm & 2-6pm Sat & Sun), an Art Nouveau stunner that's open the first weekend of each month.

Quick-march to the military museum

The park's western end has benches among the plane trees. Alternatively, peruse the neoclassical **pavilion** designed by Victor Horta (see the boxed text below) and, next door, the 1880 'Cairo panorama' folly that grew up to become a fully-fledged **mosque** 100 years later. The road tunnel running beneath the park is an earsore, but there are plans to fully enclose it.

Imprisoned Art

The pink-marble walls and skylights of the 1889 Horta-built pavilion in Parc du Cinquantenaire were designed to showcase sculptor Jef Lambeaux's enormous relief, *Les Passions Humaines*. However, the writhing nudes that fill Lambeaux's vision so shocked their audience that the building was locked up and remains virtually impregnable to this day.

STE CATHERINE & ST GÉRY (2, B2 & B4)

It may be hard to believe considering the number of modern restaurants, stylish shops and pose-worthy drinking spots that call them home, but the districts of Ste Catherine and St Géry are the two halves of Brussels' oldest quarter. The city was founded on the site of Place St Géry, a fact that can make you pause mid-drink in one of the square's trend-of-the-minute bars. These areas, at turns quietly charming and utterly exuberant, lie side by side in the west of the city centre, across the fume-belching traffic of Boulevard Anspach from Grand Place and the opera house district.

INFORMATION

- ✉ Lower Town
- Ⓜ Ste Catherine
- Bourse premetro
- ♿ good
- ✂ Kasbah (p57)

Rockin' the Kasbah restaurant, St Géry

Ste Catherine has a peaceful, mannered air, thanks in part to the influence of beautiful churches like the **Église St Jean Baptiste au Béguinage** (p27). Its timeless atmosphere is also due to the leisurely lunches conducted on **Marché aux Poissons** (p29), a large square that doubles as a giant seafood banquet table. St Géry is more rambunctious and tries hard to keep itself amused by eating and drinking at all hours of the day, though it adopts a more intimate persona in its less disturbed backstreets. The hub of social activity here is **Place St Géry**, which becomes easier to forgive for trying so hard to look and act cool the more time you spend in the convivial uproar of its restaurants and bars.

Running elegantly between the two is **Rue Antoine Dansaert** (p30), a boulevard of sought-after fashion interspersed with ethnic, traditional and future-looking eateries.

DON'T MISS

- standing in front of the Maison de la Bellone (p25)
- setting off on a walk with absolutely no idea of where you're going
- wondering why anyone would attempt a canine version of Manneken Pis ('Zinneke', on the corner of Rue des Chartreux and Rue St Christophe)

Place St Géry at lunch time

MUSEUMS & GALLERIES

The Brussels Card (€30), sold by **Tourist Information Brussels** (TIB; 2, D5; ☎ 02 513 89 40; Hôtel de Ville, Grand Place; 9am-6pm), and by certain museums and hotels, is valid for three days and entitles the user to free admission to 30 museums, plus free use of public transport. The TIB also sells *The Must of Brussels* (€15.65), a voucher booklet allowing free admission to some prime city sights. For information on museums with free admission or admission-free afternoons, see the boxed text on p23.

Belle-Vue (1, A3) This cog in the wheel of brewing giant Interbrew claims to produce the world's biggest selection of *lambic* beers, though pundits have argued that the 'cost-effective' methods used do not qualify the end result as true *lambic*. You can drop by the brewery during the weekend, but on weekdays you must book ahead for a visit.
☎ 02 410 19 35 www.interbrew.com Quai du Hainaut, Molenbeek-St-Jean € adult/child €3.80/2.50 10am-8pm Tue-Sun, last tour starts 6pm M Comte de Flandre

Bruxella 1238 (2, C4) To see the underground remains of a 13th-century Franciscan convent, which municipal workers literally stumbled across when they were poking beneath the Bourse in 1988, go on a tour of the compact archaeological time capsule known as Bruxella 1238. Tickets and tour information are available from the Musée de la Ville de Bruxelles (p22).
☎ 02 279 43 50 Rue de la Bourse, Lower Town € adult/child/student €3/1.50/2.50 tours 10am 1st Wed each month M De Brouckère Bourse premetro

Fondation Jacques Brel (1, D4) Brussels loves Brel, so much so that it peppered 2003 with concerts and exhibitions dedicated to the passionately antibourgeois cabaret singer. The Fondation Jacques Brel keeps the man's larger-than-life spirit alive by screening footage of famous concerts – at the time of research, Brel's 1966 farewell gig at the Olympia in Paris – followed by a brief interactive documentary.
☎ 02 511 10 20 www.jacquesbrel.be Place de la Vieille Halle aux Blés 11, Lower Town € adult/student from €5/3.50 10am-5pm Tue, Wed & Fri-Sun, 10am-8pm Thu M Gare Centrale good

Maison d'Erasme This splendid, gabled house-museum milks its connection with famed philosopher Erasmus for all it's worth – he lived here for a mere five months in 1521. More than 600 items are spread over two timber-beamed floors, including coins, furniture, paintings and 16th-century editions of his books, while out back is a peaceful, rambling garden with contemporary sculptures. The house can be visited in conjunction with the nearby Musée du Béguinage (Rue du Chapelain 8); a single ticket gives access to both sites.
☎ 02 521 13 83 www.ciger.be/erasmus/house Rue du Chapitre 31, Anderlecht € €1.25, incl admission to Musée du Béguinage 10am-5pm Tue-Sun M St Guidon

Musée Antoine Wiertz (3, A3) Antoine-Joseph Wiertz was a 19th-century painter, sculptor and writer with a penchant for creating massive, grandiloquent

Maison d'Erasme

The Sax family, Musée des Instruments de Musique

canvases with theological (some would say grotesque) themes. The museum, set up in Wiertz's former studio, displays dark works such as *L'Enfant Brûlé* (The Burnt Child) and some of his less controversial portraits. **☎ 02 648 17 18 www.fine-arts-museum.be/site/EN/frames/F_wiertz.html Rue Vautier 62, EU Area € free 10am-noon & 1-5pm Tue-Fri & alternate weekends M Maelbeek**

Musée Charlier (1, F3) This Horta-renovated townhouse was once the home of 19th-century sculptor Guillaume Charlier, who packed it with distinguished artworks. It's now a museum of decorative and applied arts, which exhibits fine paintings, antique furniture, tapestries and porcelain. It was undergoing extensive renovations when we visited. **☎ 02 218 53 82 www.charliermuseum.be (French & Dutch only) Ave des Arts 16, Upper Town € €5 noon-5pm Tue-Sat M Madou**

Musée Constantin Meunier (Map p33) Twenty metres down Rue de 'l'Abbaye from its intersection with Chaussée de Vleurgat is this engrossing gallery of sculptures and paintings by Constantin Meunier. A chronicler of the working class, Meunier produced often-grim representations of people bearing great burdens. Highlights include the hall of large, emotive sculptures and glimpses of the beautiful garden out back. **☎ 02 648 44 49, 02 508 32 11 www.fine-arts-museum.be/site/EN/frames/F_meunier.html Rue de l'Abbaye 59, Ixelles € free 10am-noon & 1-5pm Tue-Fri & alternate weekends M Louise, then tram No 93 or 94**

Musée de la Ville de Bruxelles (2, D5) This capital museum is spread over three floors of the stunning neo-Gothic Maison du Roi, where it evokes Brussels' past through an array of paintings, sculptures, intricate city models, books and other historical ephemera. There's also a changing roster of interesting temporary exhibits and a quirky Manneken Pis fancy-dress gallery. **☎ 02 279 43 50 Grand Place, Lower Town € adult/child/student €3/1.50/2.50 10am-5pm Tue-Fri, 10am-1pm Sat & Sun M De Brouckère Bourse premetro**

Musée des Instruments de Musique (1, E4) Within the sublime Art Nouveau confines of the Old England building is a magnificent collection of instruments: serpentine horns, 17th-century harps and guitars, bazooka-shaped flutes and overwrought pianos, many of which can be sampled through temperamental wireless headsets. Allow a few hours to explore, then check out the view from the 6th-floor restaurant. **☎ 02 545 01 30 www.mim.fgov.be Rue Montagne de la Cour 2, Upper Town € adult/concession/child under 12 €5/3.50/free 9.30am-5pm Tue, Wed & Fri, 9.30am-8pm Thu, 10am-5pm Sat & Sun M Gare Centrale excellent**

Musée d'Ixelles This is an absorbing gallery with a permanent display of 19th- and 20th-century art, including works by Magritte and Meunier. It also invites some excellent short-term exhibitions; a recent example was the Heinrich Simon private collection of modern Belgian art. Admission prices vary depending on which exhibition is in the spotlight. **☎ 02 515 64 22 musee.ixelles@skynet.be Rue Jean Van Volsem 71, Ixelles € adult/concession**

€6.20/4.95 ⏲ 1-6.30pm Tue-Fri, 10am-5pm Sat & Sun Ⓜ Porte de Namur 🚊 No 81 or 82 ♿ good

Musée du Cacao et du Chocolat (2, D6)
Despite the dreary cocoa harvesting/processing displays and cheapskate 'complimentary' tasting (a single choc-dipped biscuit), this museum of confection is worth a quick browse for its collection of old chocolate boxes and moulds, and for the downstairs demonstrations of praline-making. Also check out what appears to be edible fashion upstairs. **☎ 02 514 20 48 💻 www.mucc.be ✉ Grand Place 13, Lower Town € adult/child under 12/concession €5/free/4 ⏲ 10am-5pm Tue-Sun Ⓜ De Brouckère 🚊 Bourse premetro**

Musée du Cinéma (1, E4)
This museum has a small, thoughtful exhibit on film-making, including some fascinating old equipment. But of greater interest to old-movie buffs are the regular screenings of lauded films, from Fellini's *La Dolce Vita* to Chaplin's *The Tramp*, with some silent movies accompanied by live piano. Bookings are highly recommended; pick up a programme at the museum. **☎ 02 507 83 70 💻 www.cinematheque.be (French & Dutch only) ✉ Palais des Beaux-Arts, Rue Baron Horta 9 € free; movie admission €2 ⏲ 10am-5pm Tue-Fri, plus film screenings Ⓜ Parc ♿ good**

Musée du Cinquantenaire (3, C2) Worldwide history and art is the sweeping theme of this collection, located in the Cinquantenaire complex's southern wing. It includes artefacts from sundry ancient civilisations, as well as sections on national archaeology and European decorative arts. The museum was being extensively renovated at the time of research, so exhibits may change. **☎ 02 741 72 11 💻 www.kmkg-mrah.be (French & Dutch only) ✉ Parc du Cinquantenaire 10, EU Area € permanent collection adult/child/concession €4/1.50/3 ⏲ 9.30am-5pm Tue-Fri, 10am-5pm Sat & Sun Ⓜ Mérode ♿ good**

Musée René Magritte
The unassuming house where Magritte lived for nearly a quarter-century from 1930 has been carefully restored and has an abundance of old photos and papers relating to the surrealist artist. Some of his reality-twisting works are displayed, though all are copies. Magritte daubed more than 800 paintings here, a number of them incorporating elements of the house and the street outside. **☎ 02 428 26 26 ✉ Rue Esseghem 135, Jette € €6 ⏲ 10am-6pm Wed-Sun Ⓜ Belgica, then tram No 19**

Musées Bellevue (1, E4)
The Museum of the Dynasty, devoted to Belgium's royal lineage, is in the former Bellevue Hotel, itself built on the ruins of the 11th-century Coudenberg Palace. After browsing the fusty particulars of each monarch's reign and the sombre King Baudouin Memorial, dedicated to the popular king who died unexpectedly in 1993, you can descend to the Coudenberg archaeological site. **☎ 02 545 08 00 💻 www.musbellevue.be ✉ Place des Palais 7, Upper Town € museum adult/child under 12/student €3/free/2; Coudenberg €4/free/3; museum & Coudenberg €5/free/4 ⏲ 10am-6pm Tue-Sun Apr-Sep, 10am-5pm Tue-Sun Oct-Mar Ⓜ Parc ♿ fair**

Budget Culture

A number of Brussels' premier museums are kind enough to let the general public rampage through their precious collections for free from 1pm onwards on the first Wednesday of every month. Participants in this exhibition of goodwill include the Musée des Instruments de Musique, the Muséum des Sciences Naturelles de Belgique, the Musées Royaux des Beaux-Arts de Belgique and the Musée du Cinquantenaire. Going one better, institutions such as the Musée Antoine Wiertz and the Musée Constantin Meunier are free every day.

NOTABLE BUILDINGS & MONUMENTS

Arcade du Cinquantenaire (3, D2) The Parc du Cinquantenaire's triple -arched centrepiece and its two wings were built to celebrate the 50th anniversary of Belgian independence in 1880, but weren't completed until 1905. Look up beyond the flag in the central arch to the Thomas Vinçotte horse-drawn sculpture – admire it from the west to avoid an eyeful of brassy equine derrières.
✉ **Parc du Cinquantenaire, EU Area** Ⓜ **Mérode** ♿ **good**

Atomium (Map p35) This famous replica of an iron molecule on steroids, built for the 1958 World Fair, is now a tad dishevelled, but targeted for an intensive cleanup and reorganisation throughout 2004. Current visits are trippy, *2001: A Space Odyssey* experiences where you're subjected to a disorienting swirl of lights, sounds and images that apparently portray the Atomium's history.
☎ **02 475 47 75** 💻 **www.atomium.be** ✉ **Square de l'Atomium, Laeken** € **adult/child €6/3** 🕑 **9am-8pm Apr-Aug, 10am-6pm Sep-Mar** Ⓜ **Heysel**

Berlaymont (3, B1) Possibly only a city so preoccupied with bureaucracy could conceive of a massive, four-pointed building to house the European Commission elite (in 1967), evacuate it due to an oversupply of poisonous asbestos (in 1991) and then spend over a decade trying to clean it up. As the cleanup continues, a dozen metal-and-glass storeys sit unoccupied on prime EU real estate.
✉ **Rond-Point Robert Schuman, EU Area** Ⓜ **Schuman**

Bourse (2, C4) The frieze-festooned, lion-guarded, neoclassical cube that houses the Belgian Stock Exchange was built in 1873 according to a blueprint drafted by Léon-Pierre Suys, with Auguste Rodin adding some of the sculptures on the southwestern facade. This white-collar hive now serves as much as a city-centre landmark for tourists as the country's share-trading hub.
✉ **Place de la Bourse, Lower Town** Ⓜ **De Brouckère** 🚋 **Bourse premetro**

Colonne du Congrès (1, E3) Guarded by a pair of impressive bronze lions, this 50m-high Joseph Poelaert–designed column was raised in 1850 to commemorate the constitution-proclaiming National Congress held 19 years earlier. Its length is bookended at the bottom by an 'eternal' flame, burning in memory of Belgians killed in both world wars, and at the top by a statue of Léopold I.
✉ **Place du Congrès, Upper Town** Ⓜ **Botanique** ♿ **good**

European Parliament (3, A3) Guided tours of the lofty, domed European Parliament, nicknamed Caprice des Dieux (Whim of the Gods), are yawn-stifling affairs, mostly spent in the enormous hemicycle (debating chamber) listening to a recorded monologue on an mp3 headset. Still, you get to see the epicentre of European politics, and the information centre has plenty of background material on EU workings.
☎ **02 284 37 92** 💻 **www.europarl.eu.int/brussels (French, Dutch & German only)** ✉ **Rue Wiertz 60, EU Area** € **tours free** 🕑 **information centre 9am-5.15pm Mon-Fri; tours 10am & 3pm Mon-Thu, 10am Fri** Ⓜ **Maelbeek** ♿ **excellent**

Flying the Flag

The little blue flag with a circle of 12 five-pointed gold stars that was on the licence plate of the car that just ran over your toes is the official symbol of the allmighty European Union. If you want to indulge in some symbolic power-sharing, pop down to **Eurolines** (2, E5; ☎ 02 511 36 30; Rue du Marché aux Herbes 52, Lower Town), where you can snap up EU flag–decorated mouse pads, cups, lighters, t-shirts, soccer balls, euro-shaped letter openers...

Hôtel de Ville (2, D5)
A 'hôtel' in the sense of a still-functioning town hall rather than somewhere you can order room service, this superb Gothic building has a 96m-high spire topped by a golden weather vane in the shape of St Michel, Brussels' patron saint. Tours (30 minutes) of the interior take in 15th-century Flemish tapestries, pompous portraiture and several immodest Louis XIV-style council chambers.
☎ 02 548 04 45 ✉ Grand Place, Lower Town € tours €3 ⏲ tours 3.15pm Tue & Wed, plus 10.45am & 12.15pm Sun Apr-Sep M De Brouckère 🚊 Bourse premetro ♿ good

Maison de la Bellone (2, A2) The magnificent 17th-century facade of the Maison de la Bellone can be found at the end of an arcade off Rue de Flandre, where it's protected from the elements under a glass canopy. The house took its name from the goddess of war, Bellona, a statue of whom sits above the main door.
✉ Rue de Flandre 46, Lower Town € free ⏲ 10am-6pm Tue-Fri Aug-Jun M Ste Catherine ♿ fair

Maison de la Bellone

Manneken Pis (2, C6)
This is an iconic yet rather underwhelming 30cm-high statuette of a naked boy pissing in the street, a scene tourists feel mysteriously compelled to capture on video. The bronze tyke captures the city's irreverent spirit, particularly when clothed by locals: he's been dressed up to look like everyone from a postman to (apparently) John Malkovich.
💻 www.mannekenpis.be ✉ cnr Rue de l'Étuve & Rue du Chêne, Lower Town M Gare Centrale 🚊 Bourse premetro ♿ good

Palais de Justice (1, C6)
It took 17 years and the death of architect Joseph Poelaert to build this mighty temple of law. Stand in the enormous interior forecourt and stare up into the sky-scraping 100m-high dome. A large elevator in the square below whisks people 20m straight up from the Marolles to Place Poelaert, from where there are fine views of Lower Town rooftops.
☎ 02 508 61 11 ✉ Place Poelaert, Upper Town € free ⏲ 8.30am-5pm Mon-Fri M Louise ♿ good

Palais Royal (1, E5) For just over a month each year, the royal 'haves' fling open the doors of their official Brussels home to let the 'have-nots' take a peek. Don't pass up the opportunity to tour the *palais*, built on the site of the Coudenberg Palace, to see its rococo drawing rooms, lavish Hall of Mirrors and

Palais de Justice

the towering, unforgettable Throne Room.
☎ 02 551 20 20 ✉ Place des Palais, Upper Town € free ⏲ 10.30am-4.30pm Tue-Sun mid-July–early Sep M Parc ♿ excellent

Porte de Hal (1, B6) Porte de Hal looks like a castle that's been squeezed in a giant compactor. It's the sole surviving gateway out of the seven that were slotted into the city's second perimeter wall in the 14th century. A clump of ivy smothers the southern side of the tower, once used as a prison but now housing temporary historical exhibitions.
✉ Blvd du Midi, St Gilles M Porte de Hal ♿ good

Tour d'Angle (1, D4)
For an up-close look at the original wall that encircled the city in the 12th century, check out the Tour d'Angle (Corner Tower), one of 50 defensive towers that reared up along the wall's 4km length. For an interesting architectural contrast, see the bowling alley next door.
✉ Blvd de l'Empereur, Upper Town M Gare Centrale ♿ good

CHURCHES & CATHEDRALS

Admission to churches in Brussels is usually free, though an admission fee is charged for most concerts.

Basilique Nationale de Koekelberg The design of this enormous basilica, a part neo-Gothic, part Art Deco sandstone monolith that's ranked as the world's fifth-largest church, alternately provokes groans of admiration and loathing from visitors. Climb 240 steps (or catch the lift) to arrive partway up the 90m-high verdigris dome for a bird's-eye view of Brussels.
☎ 02 425 88 22 ✉ Parvis de la Basilique 1, Koekelberg € admission to basilica free; panorama adult/student €2.50/2 ⌚ 9am-5pm May-Oct, 10am-4pm Nov-Apr Ⓜ Simonis

Église Notre Dame de la Chapelle (1, C5) The otherwise bland Place de la Chapelle yields this interesting Romanesque and Gothic hybrid, completed in the 13th century and thus the city's oldest church. Feast your eyes on the baroque altar in the Chapel of the Rosary and the resting place of Pieter Breugel the Elder, buried here in 1569; his son supplied the funerary monument in the side chapel.
☎ 02 512 07 37 ✉ Rue des Ursulines 4, Marolles Ⓜ Gare Centrale 🚊 Anneessens premetro

Église Notre Dame du Finistère (1, D2) Sitting demurely opposite the concrete retail vault of Inno, this 17th-century baroque chapel has a gorgeous alabaster interior decorated with marble pillars, a starry ceiling, some lovely stained-glass images and a splendid organ fixed above the entrance. The organ regularly tunes up for free concerts, usually held on Mondays at 12.45pm.
☎ 02 217 52 52 ✉ Rue Neuve, Lower Town Ⓜ De Brouckère ♿ good

Église Notre Dame du Sablon (1, D5) This late-Gothic construction, begun by a guild of crossbow enthusiasts at the start of the 14th century, is admirable for its size, the sculpted pulpit, the baroque chapels flanking the choir and the beautiful collection of stained-glass windows, particularly the waterfall of colour behind the main altar.
☎ 02 511 57 41 ✉ Rue de la Régence 3b, Sablon Ⓜ Porte de Namur ♿ fair

Basilique Nationale de Koekelberg

Église Ste Catherine (2, B2) Built in the mid-19th century by Joseph Poelaert, who later designed the Palais de Justice, this stylistic mishmash has a stony, prayer-weathered interior. Inspect the 15th-century black Madonna, the pulpit and, above the entrance, Theodore van Loon's *The Nativity*. Next door is a 17th-century belfry once attached to a now-defunct 15th-century church.
☎ 02 513 34 81 ✉ Place Ste Catherine, Lower Town Ⓜ Ste Catherine

Église St Jacques sur Coudenberg (1, E5) This beautiful church has an imposing Corinthian-columned entrance, but a refreshingly underwrought interior. Its neoclassical style dates from 1785 and it contains Jan Portaels paintings, a Laurent Delvaux statue of St Joseph and a striking 19th-century Spanish Madonna statue. You can catch various free concerts here.
☎ 02 511 78 36 ✉ Place Royale, Upper Town ⌚ 1-6pm Tue-Sat, 9am-6pm Sun Ⓜ Trône

The Begijnen

In the 12th century, women of the Low Countries who were either unmarried or widowed as a result of the man-depleting Crusades began to band together in Catholic communities called *begijnhoven* (*béguinage* in French) where, as *begijnen* (or Beguines), they adhered to religious vows and worked to keep the all-female community independent. A *begijnhof* was usually a wall-encircled grouping of small houses sharing a central garden and church. You can visit one of the few still-functioning *begijnhof* in Bruges (p36) and explore a former Beguine convent in Anderlecht (Musée du Béguinage; p21).

Église St Jean Baptiste au Béguinage (2, C1) Erected in the 17th century to receive the worship of what was then the largest Beguine community in Belgium (see the boxed text above), this church stands out for the baroque touches applied by architect Luc Fayd'Herbe, a pupil of Rubens, and for its restoration after a devastating fire in 2000. Try to see the beautiful triple-gabled facade when it's floodlit at night.
☎ 02 217 87 42 ✉ Place du Béguinage, Lower Town Ⓜ Ste Catherine ♿ good

Église St Nicolas (2, D4) The interesting church of St Nicolas, the patron saint of merchants, is fittingly buried amid a jumble of shops on a site that it has occupied since the 14th century. The interior artworks are attributed to Pieter Paul Rubens and Bernard van Orley, while the curious angle of the church's three aisles is apparently due to efforts to fit the chapel around an old watercourse.
☎ 02 511 26 38 ✉ Rue au Beurre 1, Lower Town Ⓜ De Brouckère 🚊 Bourse premetro

Église Sts Pierre et Guidon This massive, 14th-century Gothic construction is worth the metro ride out to Anderlecht. It features the polished splendour of the Shrine of St Guidon (the patron saint of peasants), which is topped by four saintly silver statuettes. After visiting the church, stroll down narrow, charming Rue Porselein, which lies opposite the church entrance; it's one of the oldest streets in Brussels' oldest suburb.
✉ Place de la Vaillance, Anderlecht Ⓜ St Guidon

PARKS & GARDENS

Bois de la Cambre (4, C3) This stroll-worthy chunk of forest is a slender extension of the much larger Forêt de Soignes (see below) that blankets the earth to the southeast of Brussels. You'll find a serene array of lakes and parkland, as well as a meditative 12th-century monastery called Abbaye de la Cambre.
✉ Bois de la Cambre, Ixelles 🚊 No 93 or 94 ♿ fair

Forêt de Soignes (4, C3) The northeastern branch of Brussels' largest swath of greenery is best reached on foot by following the signage off Avenue Herrmann-Debroux, across the road from the similarly named metro station. Besides providing lots of beech trees to hug and some lovely *étangs* (ponds) to sit around, the forest also contains the Rouge Cloître, a 14th-century abbey.
☎ Rouge Cloître information centre 02 629 34 11 ✉ Forêt de Soignes,

Bloomin' Beauties

Situated just off Avenue du Parc Royal on the edge of the Domaine Royal (Royal Estate) in Laeken is a series of huge greenhouses, the **Serres Royales** (Map p35). These magisterial 19th-century enclosures house a wondrous floral community, including fuchsias, camellias, rare trees and many tropical plants. The antique hothouses are open to the public for 10 days each year (normally mid-April to early May; adult/child €2/free), when plant-lovers form impressive queues to poke their heads inside. One of the days is reserved for people with disabilities. To reach the site by public transport, take bus No 53. For more information, visit the TIB.

Auderghem ⏲ 2-6pm Tue-Sun May-Oct, 2-5pm Tue-Sun Nov-Apr M Herrmann-Debroux 🚌 No 95 from the Bourse

Le Botanique (1, F2)
This is a captivating series of formal terraces hidden behind the French Community Cultural Centre (p67), with Meunier statuary, minihedges and a fountain for company. The striking neoclassical glass rotunda was part of the city's original botanical gardens, which packed up and moved to Meise (p37) in the early 19th century.
✉ Rue Royale, St Josse ⏲ 8am-5pm Oct-Apr, 7am-8pm May-Sep M Botanique ♿ fair

Parc de Bruxelles (1, E4)
Brussels' most popular outdoor promenade is filled with benches and mature trees, and pierced by wide gravel paths. Buy an ice cream from the kiosk near the statue-ringed fountain, admire the old bandstand, or just sprawl on the grass and contemplate the human traffic.
✉ Parc de Bruxelles, Upper Town M Parc ♿ good

Parc de Laeken (Map p35)
This expansive patchwork of tree groves and rolling open ground lies opposite the out-of-bounds royal estate, and is good for spreading out picnics or spontaneous games of football. In the centre of the park is a lofty neo-Gothic statue of Léopold I, while hidden nearby in the foliage is the Villa Belvédère, a fenced-off royal hideaway.
✉ Parc de Laeken, Laeken M Heysel ♿ fair

Parc des Bruxelles

Parc Léopold (3, A3)
This is a cultivated patch of parkland that stretches out behind the European Parliament, dotted with trees and usually filled with a natural hush. Extensive recent landscaping should ensure that stressed Eurocrats have some nice open areas in which to have quality postmeeting tantrums.
✉ Parc Léopold, EU Area M Maelbeek ♿ fair

Square Marie-Louise (3, A1) This is not a 'square' in the conventional sense of the word, considering it's shaped like a pair of underpants and 90% of it is filled with water. Nonetheless, this sizeable tree-ringed pond is a good place to catch your breath. Try to make sense of the grotto at its eastern end and the stunted volcano afloat in the middle.
✉ Square Marie-Louise, EU Area M Maelbeek ♿ fair

PLACES & STREETS

Avenue Louise (1, D6) The twinkling Cartier outlet at its northern end sums up this avenue's high-class retail character, though the Quick hamburger joint opposite tries to undermine it. Shoppers luxuriate in their own reflections in the windows of Gucci, Caroline Biss and Lancel (of Paris, of course). The boutiques thin out as you sashay further south from Place Stéphanie.
✉ Ave Louise, Ixelles Ⓜ Louise ♿ good

Avenue Palmerston (3, B1) This broad, nicely manicured thoroughfare slopes down from the attractive flower beds and fountains of Square Ambiorix to the watery expanse of Square Marie-Louise, negotiating well-heeled suburbia along the way. It makes a refreshing change from the gritty clutter of the centre. While you're here, enjoy the Art Nouveau character of Maison St-Cyr (Square Ambiorix 11) and Hôtel Van Eetvelde (Avenue Palmerston 2-4).
✉ Ave Palmerston, EU Area Ⓜ Schuman ♿ good

Marché aux Poissons (2, B1) Also called Vismet, this elongated stretch of tree-lined paving was once the city's harbour and site of a lively fish market. The fishy theme is continued nowadays by the fine seafood restaurants operating from beside the old quays and setting up breezy à la carte marquees in the square.

Place du Petit Sablon

✉ Marché aux Poissons, Lower Town Ⓜ Ste Catherine ♿ good

Place des Martyrs (2, F2) This low-key little square is dedicated to the 467 patriots who died during the Belgian revolt against the Dutch in 1830 – their graves lie under the central statue. It's shielded from city noise by a perimeter of two-storey buildings and so is a good place to collect (or scatter) your thoughts, though beware the sharply uneven cobblestones on your way in.
✉ Place des Martyrs, Lower Town Ⓜ De Brouckère

Place du Grand Sablon (1, D5) This is a chichi pedestrian zone (albeit marred by a large car park) where uptown dogs walk their handlers and reserved, formally attired couples sit at expensive outdoor cafés and squint fiercely at all the tourists. It's also the vortex of the city's antiques trade, with estimable dealerships scattered throughout the surrounding streets.
✉ Place du Grand Sablon, Upper Town Ⓜ Porte de Namur ♿ good

Place du Petit Sablon (1, D5) This lovely, miniature, formal garden was planted in 1890 and is fenced in by a balustrade topped by 48 Paul Hankar-designed bronze statues, one for each of Belgium's medieval guilds. Despite its exposure to city noise and the rather stuffy fountain-anchored statue of Counts Egmont and Hoorn, the garden is more than amenable to an extended sit-down.
✉ Place du Petit Sablon, Upper Town Ⓜ Porte de Namur ♿ fair

Place Royale (1, E4) Palatial, white, neoclassical buildings – among them the Église St Jacques sur Coudenberg (p26) and the rump of the Musées Royaux des Beaux-Arts de Belgique (p18) – surround a busy cobblestoned roundabout with a statue of 11th-century hero Godefroid de Bouillon at its centre. The Old England building (p22) peeks out enigmatically from behind another edifice down a side street.
✉ Place Royale, Upper Town Ⓜ Parc ♿ good

Place Ste Catherine (2, B2) This peaceful, relatively untrammelled square stretches out on either side of Église Ste Catherine. After browsing the local fruit and vegetable market, claim a bench and look out over the paving stones to the row of houses on the northern side, which includes a cream-coloured 1759 abode that abuts some attractive younger buildings, many now housing restaurants.
✉ Place Ste Catherine, Lower Town Ⓜ Ste Catherine ♿ good

Rue Antoine Dansaert (2, A2) Since the mid-1980s, a gaggle of high-fashion stores and smart restaurants has been forming at the southern end of this *rue*, their contemporary gloss providing a stark contrast to the 19th-century buildings around them. The better-known outlets include Stijl and Olivier Strelli (both p41).
✉ Rue Antoine Dansaert, Lower Town Ⓜ Ste Catherine ♿ good

Street Talk

Brussels has some peculiarly long street signs, along the lines of 'Petite Rue de la Violette Korte Violetstraat'. This is because each sign must include both the French and Flemish names, with the French name coming first. So, in the above example, 'Petite Rue de la Violette' is the French name and 'Korte Violetstraat' is the Flemish. Also note that in French, *rue* (street) comes at the start of a name, while the Flemish *straat* is tacked onto the end. We've gone with French street names throughout this book for simplicity's sake; no offence to Flemish readers is intended.

Rue des Bouchers (2, E4) Walk through this narrow, cobblestoned *rue* at meal times only if you're prepared for a tug-of-war with waiters eager to pull you into one of the multitude of restaurants piled up on the footpaths (see the boxed text on p50). For more of the same, squeeze through the even thinner Petite Rue des Bouchers. These streets are worth seeing at night when fairy lights come out to play.
✉ Rue des Bouchers, Lower Town Ⓜ De Brouckère ♿ fair

Rue Neuve (2, E2) This is Brussels' main pedestrianised shopping zone, a teeming strip of retail combat that knows it can't compete with prestige-hungry Avenue Louise, hence the medium-priced sales pitch. The stretch of Rue Neuve just shy of Rue du Fossé aux Loups is where you'll find the biggest concentration of recognisable clothing and accessories outlets.
✉ Rue Neuve, Lower Town Ⓜ De Brouckère ♿ good

QUIRKY BRUSSELS

Bruxelles les Bains (1, C1) In August 2003, copying a trend started in other landlocked European cities, Brussels trucked lots of sand in from the coast, dumped it next to a canal and declared the city's new beach officially open (albeit for only one month). It's hoped the pretend *plage* (beach) and its mock-Polynesian foodstalls, concerts and sports competitions (volleyball, *pétanque*) becomes an annual event.
☎ 02 279 50 29 ✉ Quai des Péniches, St Josse € free 🕓 11am-7pm Wed & Thu, 11am-10pm Fri-Sun Aug Ⓜ Yser ♿ fair

Cerceuil (2, E5) This crypt-sized bar does its best with beyond-the-grave gimmickry, including coffin tables, skull mugs and cocktails called 'sperme' and 'urine'. Admittedly the novelty wears off pretty quickly after you've spilled beer on yourself three times while reaching for your glass in the near-impenetrable gloom.
☎ 02 512 30 77 ✉ Rue des Harengs 10-12, Lower Town 🕓 4pm-2am Sun-Tue, 11am-late Wed-Sat Ⓜ De Brouckère 🚊 Bourse premetro

Hair Club (2, A6) This fancy-dress department store has something for every occasion, no matter how odd. Get fitted out in glam, ghoul, girlie, groovy, ga-ga or go-go costumes and wigs, to rent or to buy as a keepsake. Professional-strength make-up is also available. Look for the big chapeau out front.
☎ 02 511 41 93 🖳 www.hairclub.be ✉ Boulevard Anspach 153, Lower Town ⏲ 9.30am-6.30pm Mon-Fri, 10am-6pm Sat Ⓜ De Brouckère 🚊 Bourse premetro

Jeanneke Pis (2, E4) Behind every little boy is a little girl. This sister statue to Manneken Pis may have seemed like a good idea when it was erected 20 years ago, but her waterworks were off when we visited and few visitors were tempting luck by dropping a euro into the stagnant basin at her feet.
✉ Impasse de la Fidélité, Lower Town Ⓜ De Brouckère 🚊 Bourse premetro ♿ good

Statue of Everard 't Serclaes

Statue of Everard 't Serclaes (2, D6) The wall-mounted bronze statue on Rue Charles Buls that's constantly being fondled by grinning passers-by represents the heroic Everard 't Serclaes, who was murdered while defending Brussels' honour in the 14th century. It's believed that rubbing the statue's arm brings good luck – hopefully not the luck that abandoned poor Everard in his hour of need.
✉ Rue Charles Buls, Lower Town Ⓜ De Brouckère 🚊 Bourse premetro ♿ good

BRUSSELS FOR CHILDREN

Brussels' many child-friendly sights and activities are outlined in various tourist publications available from the TIB. Eating out with kids is fine in casual places but not in top-end eateries; note that many cafés and pubs can be thick with smoke. Reviews in this book's Eating, Entertainment and Sleeping chapters tagged with the 🚸 icon denote places with highchairs and/or kid-sized meals, entertainment suitable for kids, and sleeping cots. Also see the 'For Children' section of the Shopping chapter (p44).

AeroBrussels Give the kids a thrill by bundling them into a giant helium balloon that gets winched via the attached cable to a height of 150m above the Gare du Nord. It's not a cheap thrill, however, when you consider the paltry 10-minute 'flight' time.
☎ 02 201 30 30 🖳 www.aerophile.com ✉ Espace Gaucheret (off Blvd Roi Albert II), Schaerbeek € adult/child/student €10/5/8 ⏲ 10am-6pm daily Oct-Apr, 9am-7pm Sun-Wed & 9am-9pm Thu-Sat May-Sep Ⓜ Gare du Nord ♿ fair

Bruparck (Map p35) Bruparck is a sprawling, ultra commercial amusement complex, every square inch plastered with cash-hungry attractions. Within the park's boundaries are Mini-Europe, with 300 miniature reproductions of famous sites; the slippery waterslides of Océade (p32); a planetarium; the Kinepolis cinemas (p64); and a grouping of overpriced eateries called The Village.
☎ 02 474 83 77 🖳 www.bruparck.com ✉ Blvd du Centenaire 20, Laeken € entry free, separate admission prices for all attractions ⏲ from 9.30am Ⓜ Heysel ♿ good

Science, naturally

Muséum des Sciences Naturelles de Belgique (3, A3) An old-fashioned natural history museum housed in an enormous pavilion, this place is loads of fun and heavy on the educational front too. Face off with colossal, eerily-lit iguanodon skeletons and a menagerie of glassy-eyed pelts from around the world. If you're craving something living, the creepy-crawly community in the upstairs vivarium is busy doing just that.
☎ 02 627 42 38 🖳 **www.naturalsciences.be** ✉ **Rue Vautier 29, EU Area** € **permanent exhibition adult/child/concession €4/1.50/3** 🕒 **9.30am-4.45pm Tue-Fri, 10am-6pm Sat & Sun** Ⓜ **Maelbeek** ♿ **good**

Océade (Map p35)
Unleash the family in this fun aquatic park. Go shooting down the Cannonball, Cyclone or Kamikaze waterslides (they're safer than they sound), bob across the indoor pool in a large buoy, sweat it out in 'sauna land', or just slouch in a deckchair. Tickets give you four hours' access.
☎ 02 478 43 20 🖳 **www.oceade.be (French & Dutch only)** ✉ **Bruparck, Blvd du Centenaire 20, Laeken** € **adult/child €13/10.50** 🕒 **10am-6pm Tue-Fri, 10am-10pm Sat & Sun Apr-Jun; 10am-10pm daily Jul & Aug; 10am-6pm Wed-Fri, 10am-10pm Sat & Sun Sep-Mar** Ⓜ **Heysel** ♿ **good**

Scientastic Museum (2, C4)
Secreted under the Bourse is this subterranean science lab, containing around 80 hands-on science displays. The enterprisingly low-tech exhibits put all five human senses to the test and should keep the kids interested for at least a few milliseconds, perhaps even longer.
☎ 02 732 13 36 🖳 **www.scientastic.be** ✉ **Bourse premetro station, Lower Town** € **adult/child €5/4** 🕒 **12.30-2pm Mon-Fri, 2-5.30pm Sat, Sun & school holidays** Ⓜ **De Brouckère** 🚊 **Bourse premetro**

Théâtre Royal de Toone

Théâtre Royal de Toone (2, E5) This theatre's delightful wood-and-papier-mâché marionettes have been acting out tried-and-true productions of *Faust* and *Hamlet* since 1830, thanks initially to puppet pioneer Antoine ('Toone') Gente and nowadays to a seventh-generation descendant. If you need a wheelchair accommodated, let the theatre know when ordering tickets.
☎ 02 511 71 37 🖳 **www.toone.be** ✉ **Impasse Schuddeveld 6 (Petite Rue des Bouchers 21), Lower Town** € **adult/child €10/7** 🕒 **shows usually 8.30pm Wed-Sat Feb-Dec, extra sessions 4pm Sat** Ⓜ **Gare Centrale** ♿ **good**

Kiddie Care

Bond van Grote en van Jonge Gezinnen (1, F6; ☎ 02 507 88 11; Rue du Trône 125, Ixelles) is a family-focused enterprise with a long history throughout Flanders. If you need a baby-sitter, contact the Brussels branch during normal weekday working hours. Bookings must be made at least two days in advance. To peruse other baby-sitting possibilities, look under 'Baby-sitting' in the index at the front of the local Yellow Pages (Pages d'Or; www.pagesdor.be). Most top-end hotels can arrange childcare.

WALKING TOURS
Alfresco Art Nouveau

After alighting on Avenue Louise, walk south to No 346, the Horta-sculpted **Hôtel Hallet** (**1**). Backtrack and turn right on Rue Vilain XIV, where Nos 9 and 11 host sgraffito-decorated **Antoine Blérot edifices** (**2**). Turn the corner onto Avenue du Général de Gaulle to another **Blérot pairing** (**3**) at Nos 38 and 39. Head along the *étang* (pond) and turn left on Rue du Lac to admire **Ernest de Lune's stained-glass beauty** (**4**) at No 6 before rejoining Avenue Louise. Lovers of proletarian art can detour south down Chaussée de Vleurgat, then left on Rue de l'Abbaye to **Musée Constantin Meunier** (**5**; p22). Otherwise, head citywards to Avenue Louise 224, Horta's **Hôtel Solvay** (**6**). Further north, cross into Rue Paul Émile Janson for Horta's **Hôtel Tassel** (**7**) at No 6. Take the next left on Rue de Livourne to buy a healthy snack at **La Tsampa** (**8**; p51), then reverse direction and turn left down Rue Defacqz to two Paul Hankar houses: **Maison Ciamberlani** (**9**) at No 48 and **Maison Hankar** (**10**) at No 71. Double back and turn right on Rue Faider to **Albert Roosenboom's simple creation** (**11**) at No 83. Back on Rue Defacqz, head west to Chaussée de Charleroi, then left to the brilliant **Musée Horta** (**12**; p16). While you are strolling to Horta premetro station, divert to **Moeder Lambic** (**13**; p63) for a well-deserved brew.

Sgraffito decorations

The sinuous curves of Hôtel Solvay

distance 3.6km **duration** 2½hrs
start Ⓜ Louise, then tram No 93 or 94 to stop Vleurgat
end Horta premetro

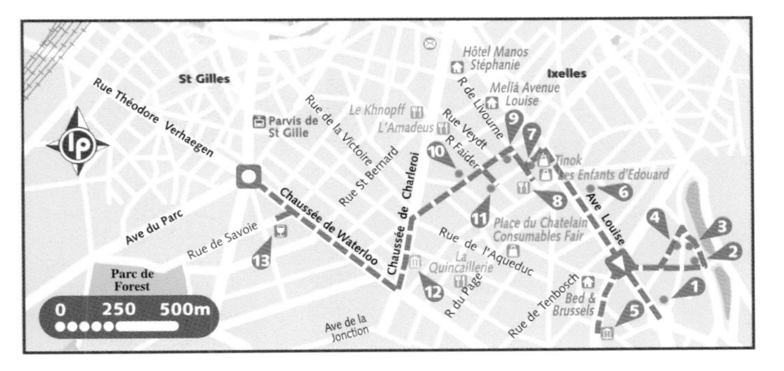

Comic Art

Pick up some comics at Pêle-Mêle

This is a slimmed-down version of the city's official 6km Comic Strip Route (visit the TIB for details). Start at Place St Géry with Marc Sleen's popular character **Nero** (**1**). Round the corner on Rue des Chartreux is Yslaire's whimsical **L'Archange** (**2**). Continue into Rue des Fabriqes for Bob De Moor's **Cori Le Moussaillon** (**3**) and Hermann's fantastical **The Dreams of Nic** (**4**). Turn left down Rue de la Senne, then take the second left to see Morris' Western parody **Lucky Luke** (**5**). Return to Rue de la Senne and make for Rue du Petit Rempart, where Edgar P Jacobs' **Le Marque Jaune** (**6**) introduces you to Blake and Mortimer. Take Rue d'Anderlecht and turn right at Rue de la Verdure for a rendezvous with Willy Maltaite's **Isabelle** (**7**), then turn left at Boulevard Maurice Lemonnier to visit second-hand comics specialist **Pêle-Mêle** (**8**; p43). Head north, then left into Borgval for a snack attack at **Le Bar à Tapas** (**9**; p57). Backtracking, turn left at Rue du Bon Secours to see Tibet's adventurous **Ric Hochet** (**10**). Weave into Rue des Grands Carmes, past **Manneken Pis** (**11**; p25) to Dany's **Olivier Rameau** (**12**). Go up Rue du Midi, then right into Rue du Marché au Charbon for contemporary artist François Schuiten's **Le Passage** (**13**). Finally, back west down Rue du Marché au Charbon are Frank Pe's **Broussaille** (**14**) and Francis Carin's suave spy **Victor Sackville** (**15**).

Not your average council paint job

distance 1.1km **duration** 1½hrs
start Bourse premetro
end Bourse premetro

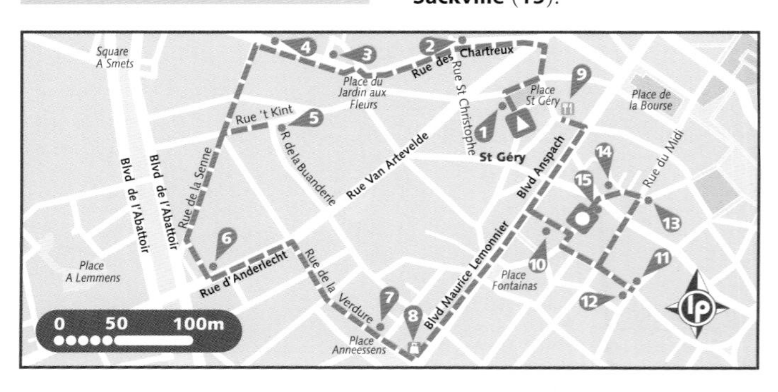

Royal Ramble

Mighty molecule: the Atomium

Once in Laeken, stand outside **Roi Baudouin Stadium** (**1**; p68) before walking down Avenue de l'Impératrice Charlotte to **Place du Belgique** (**2**) where, beyond several fountains, you'll see the statue-crowned **Parc des Expositions** (**3**). Head south down Boulevard du Centenaire and turn right into amusing **Bruparck** (**4**; p31) to fuel up on mussels at **Chez Léon** (**5**; p49). Retrace your steps to the boulevard and turn right to the molecular might of the **Atomium** (**6**; p24), then continue to Avenue du Hallier, where a left leads you into the green depths of **Parc de Laeken** (**7**; p28). Weave across grass and through copses to the Gaudi-esque hilltop **statue of Léopold I** (**8**), near the no-trespassing grounds of **Villa Belvédère** (**9**). Tumble downhill to another royal retreat, **Château Stuyvenbergh** (**10**), then walk southeast along Avenue des Trembles to the derelict **Chapelle St Anne** (**11**), hidden beside the road. Quickstep it past the royal estate's gated **Château Royal de Laeken** (**12**) to the fabulous **Serres Royales** (**13**), royal greenhouses that reveal their tropical delights to the public for just 10 days annually (see the boxed text on p28). Swing right onto Avenue Jules Van Praet and duck left into the grounds of **Pavillon Chinois** (**14**), with the **Tour Japonaise** (**15**) over the road.

Tropical treasures: the Serres Royales

distance 3.5km **duration** 2½hrs
▶ **start** Ⓜ Heysel
● **end** 🚋 No 23 to Heysel metro

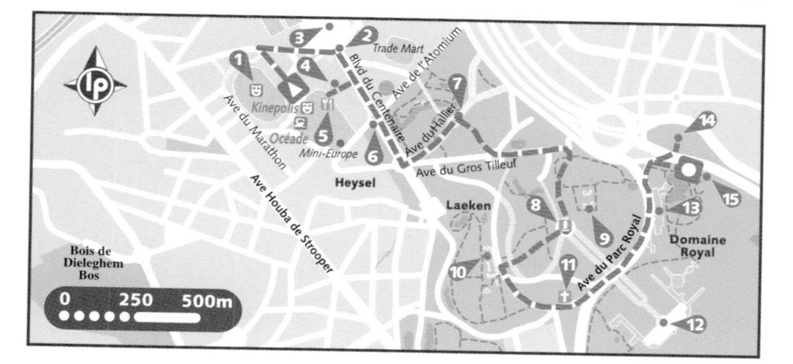

DAY TRIPS

Bruges (4, A2)

> **INFORMATION**
>
> *115km northwest of Brussels*
>
> Gare du Midi to Bruges train station (€22 return, one hour), then local bus marked 'Central' to Markt (€1, 10 minutes)
>
> www.brugge.be
>
> Brasserie Forestière (☎ 050 34 20 02; Academiestraat 15)

Bruges (Brugge in Flemish) began its life in the 9th century in the shadow of a castle built to dissuade Vikings from dropping by. By the 13th century it had developed a lucrative interest in cloth manufacturing and spent the next 300 years fêting merchants, acquiring a taste for the arts and generally stacking on the civic pounds. The silting up in the 15th century of its trade lifeline, the Zwin estuary, stopped the clock in Bruges, and the city did a Rip Van Winkle for the next four centuries. Nowadays, the well-preserved medieval ambience of this canal-riddled Flemish town draws tourists the way it used to draw traders. Start your visit early, before all the other tourists clog the narrow arteries like human cholesterol, and avoid peak-season weekends at all costs.

The most prominent feature of Bruges is the **Belfort** (Burg 11; admission adult/child €5/3; 9.30am-5pm), an 88m-high tower situated on the city's large central square, the Markt. The Belfort has a magnificent view over the city, but there are 366 steps and usually hordes of camera-toting climbers to negotiate before you can enjoy it. South of the Markt is the **Groeninge Museum** (☎ 050 44 87 43; Dijver 12; admission adult/concession €8/5; 9.30am-5pm Tue-Sun), which has a prized collection of Flemish primitive paintings, including standout works by Jan Van Eyck and Hieronymus Bosch.

A visit to the serene courtyard and whitewashed houses of the **Begijnhof** (Wijngaardplein 1; admission to grounds free; grounds 6.30am-6.30pm) is a must. And don't forget to wander aimlessly alongside Bruges' charming system of canals.

There's an **information centre** (☎ 050 44 86 86; 9.30am-6.30pm Mon-Fri, 10am-12.30pm & 2-6.30pm Sat & Sun) at Burg 11.

MARTIN MOOS

Peaceful canals and medieval architecture in Bruges

Ghent (4, B2)

Ghent (Gent in Flemish) shares the same cloth-making pedigree as Bruges, having become a European trade powerhouse by the mid-14th century and retaining a grand medieval core. But unlike Bruges, this city's historic attractions are enlivened by plenty of contemporary bustle.

The Gothic **St Baafskathedraal** (St Baafsplein; admission to altarpiece adult/child €2.50/1.25; 9.30am-5pm Mon-Sat & 1-5pm Sun Apr-Oct, 10.30am-4pm Mon-Sat & 2-5pm Sun Nov-Mar) contains Jan and Hubert Van Eyck's stunning 20-panel altarpiece, *Adoration of the Mystic Lamb*. Another highlight is **Gravensteen** (092 25 93 06; St Veerleplein; admission adult/child €6/free; 9am-6pm Apr-Sep, 9am-5pm Oct-Mar), an intimidating 12th-century castle with quintessential turrets and a moat. A clutch of fine museums, a canal cruise and trendy eateries in the Patershol quarter will complete your trip.

There's an **information centre** (092 66 52 32; 9.30am-6.30pm Apr-Oct, 9.30am-4.30pm Nov-Mar) at Botermarkt 17, in the crypt of the belfry.

INFORMATION

60km northwest of Brussels

- Gare du Midi to St Pietersstation (€13.20 return, 45 minutes), then tram No 1, 10 or 11 to Korenmarkt (€1, 10 minutes)
- www.gent.be
- Brasserie Pakhuis (092 23 55 55; Schuurkenstraat 4)

Jardin Botanique National (4, C2)

Belgium's National Botanic Garden, one of the world's largest, comprises over 93 hectares of rolling lawns, arboretums and glasshouses, naturally decorated with more than 18,000 plant specimens from around the world. It's a wonderful place to visit with a book, a picnic or just your own contemplative mind.

The Plant Palace is a series of 13 magnificent, interconnected glasshouses containing the garden's fragile and tropical inhabitants. It includes species plucked from rainforests, deserts, swamps and mountains, among them epiphytes and Peruvian fuchsias. The beautiful Balat greenhouse was built in 1854 by Alphonse Balat, who later built the Serres Royales (see the boxed text on p28), and contains giant Amazonian water lilies. Just wandering around the medicinal garden makes you feel better, and there's also the old waterfront Bouchout Castle to gawk at.

INFORMATION

12km north of Brussels

- STIB bus L from Gare du Nord to stop Meise: Bouchout Kasteel (€1.40, 25 minutes)
- 02 260 09 20
- www.br.fgov.be
- Domein van Bouchout, Meise
- adult/child under 7/concession €4/free/3
- 9am-5pm
- Orangery Tavern

ORGANISED TOURS

ARAU (1, D2) Atelier de Recherche et d'Action Urbaines (Workshop for Town-Planning Research & Action) is an urban heritage group that runs theme tours – the Marolles, Art Nouveau, suburban growth – saturated with local knowledge.
☎ **02 219 33 45** 🖳 **www.arau.org** ✉ **Blvd Adolphe Max 55, Lower Town** € **walking tour €10; coach tour €15** 🕐 **tours normally at either 10am or 2pm Sat & Sun Apr-Nov**

Brussels by Water (1, C1) Take a cruise on the city's network of old canals or sail through the waterway-threaded Belgian countryside. Refer to the brochure for the plethora of tour times.
☎ **02 203 64 06** 🖳 **www.scaldisnet.be** ✉ **Quai des Péniches 2, St Josse** € **adult/child from €6/5**

Calèches Carlos Moens-Stassens (2, D6) Draw attention to yourself by clambering aboard one of the horse-drawn buggies parked at the start of Rue Charles Buls and going for a 20-minute clatter around the Grand Place area.
☎ **053-70 05 04** ✉ **Rue Charles Buls, Lower Town** € **€18** 🕐 **Jun-Aug**

Try horsing around

Chatterbus The loquacious guides of Bus Bavard (Chatterbus) accompany you on foot or by private bus or public transport to interesting Brussels sites. Note that the weekly theme tours are conducted in French only.
☎ **02 673 18 35** 🖳 **www.busbavard.be** ✉ **Rue des Thuyas 12, Watermael-Boitsfort** € **tours from €8** 🕐 **theme tours Sat & Sun Apr-Dec**

De Boeck (2, E5) De Boeck's standard three-hour city tour buses you from Grand Place to must-sees such as the Cathédrale des Sts Michel & Gudule, the Palais Royal and the Atomium.
☎ **02 513 77 44** 🖳 **www.brussels-city-tours.com** ✉ **Rue de la Colline 8, Lower Town** € **adult/child/concession from €20/10/18**

La Fonderie (1, A2) This association of avid social historians conducts guided tours of Brussels' industrial highlights. Diverse tour themes range from the history of working-class Molenbeek-St-Jean to the city's canals and chocolate production.
☎ **02 410 99 50** 🖳 **www.lafonderie.be** ✉ **Rue Ransfort 27, Molenbeek-St-Jean** € **adult/child/student €7/4/5**

Open Tours (2, F6) Open Tours' conspicuous open-roofed double-decker buses depart from Boulevard de l'Impératrice outside Gare Centrale for a 1½-hour jaunt around the city. The 'deluxe' 2½-hour tour departs daily at 10am.
☎ **02 466 11 11** 🖳 **www.open-tours.com** ✉ **Gare Centrale, Upper Town** € **adult €12-20** 🕐 **1½-hr tours depart hourly from 10am**

Pro Velo (1, F5) This company organises pedal-powered city circuits, the majority of them 3½-hour excursions. Alternatively, hire a bike to go solo for an hour (€3), a day (€12) or a week (€60).
☎ **02 502 73 55** 🖳 **www.provelo.org** ✉ **Rue de Londres 15, Upper Town** € **tours per person from €8**

Visit Brussels Line (2, E5) Operated by De Boeck, this double-decker service departs Gare Centrale for a circuit of 14 key city sites. Tickets are valid for 24 hours; get on and off as often as you like.
☎ **02 513 77 44** 🖳 **www.brussels-city-tours.com** ✉ **Rue de la Colline 8, Lower Town** € **adult/child/concession €13.50/9/12** 🕐 **departs every 30 min 10am-4pm Mon-Fri, 10am-5pm Sat**

Shopping

Brussels has an exuberant shopping scene in which happily-fatigued consumers are continually tempted by new-season fashions (including bold Antwerp designs), stylish accessories from artful manufacturers like Delvaux, gorgeous handmade lace, elegant Art Nouveau baubles, and delicious edibles such as gourmet chocolates and monk-brewed beer. The year's main sales *(soldes)* arrive with a heavily-discounted bang in January and July.

Foreign visitors who aren't EU residents can reclaim the tax paid on purchases provided they spend a minimum of €125 in a shop with a 'Tax Free Shopping' sign, get a tax refund cheque when paying, and get the cheque stamped by customs when departing (they must exit the EU within three months of the purchase).

Shopping Areas

The classy northern end of Avenue Louise, fashion-conscious Rue Antoine Dansaert and antique-obsessed Sablon are where most of Brussels' luxury shops live. Up-market outlets also shelter in the magnificent, glass-covered Galeries St Hubert, while another notable sky-lit arcade is Passage du Nord. Mainstream shops line the Rue Neuve pedestrian strip.

ARCADES & SHOPPING CENTRES

City 2 (1, D2) Situated across Rue de la Blanchisserie from its rival Inno, this shopping centre houses many clothing, accessories and personal grooming stores, including the Body Shop, Levi's and outlets selling Hugo Boss and Versace. The top floor is engulfed by FNAC, a bazaar of electronic goods, books and music.
☎ 02 211 40 60 ✉ Rue Neuve 123, Lower Town ⌚ 10am-7pm Ⓜ Rogier

Galerie Agora (2, E6) It's a mystery how the 100-plus leather-goods shops stuffed into this winding arcade manage to stay in business, considering they all seem to be selling identical racks of ties, belts and jackets. Several shops distinguish themselves by deviating into *Barbarella*-style high-heeled glam boots.
☎ 02 513 65 72 ✉ Rue des Eperonniers, Lower Town Ⓜ Gare Centrale

Galerie d'Ixelles (1, E6) Serving Brussels' African community in Matongé is Galerie d'Ixelles, with a vastly different character from the polished lustre of mainstream arcades. It's an often-boisterous place filled with brightly patterned Congolese clothes and other African goods, and nary a Eurocrat in sight. Look for the signage on Chaussée de Wavre.
✉ Chaussée de Wavre, Ixelles Ⓜ Porte de Namur

Galeries St Hubert

Galeries Louise (1, D6) Considering the fashionable environs, this arcade is surprisingly bland, but still has a full complement of expensive clothing, accessories, and service boutiques where you can get your nails filed and your hair coiffured.
✉ Ave Louise, Ixelles ⌚ 6.30am-9.30pm Mon-Sat, 9am-9pm Sun Ⓜ Louise

Galeries St Hubert (2, F4) This is the city's most elegant shopping promenade and Europe's oldest, comprising three interconnected glass-vaulted arcades: Galerie de la Reine, Galerie du Roi and Galerie des Princes. Stroll through the colonnaded entrance into the main sky-lit neo-Renaissance space, then snaffle a treat from the up-market shops and cafés.
✉ entry at Rue du Marché aux Herbes & at Rue de l'Écuyer, Lower Town Ⓜ Gare Centrale

Passage du Nord (2, E1) Running between Rue Neuve and Boulevard Adolphe Max is this grand but egalitarian glass-covered arcade, where a 250-year-old *coutellerie* (cutlery shop) and a Davidoff outlet mix with a run-of-the-mill pharmacy and a milk bar.
02 218 50 68 Rue Neuve 40, Lower Town M De Brouckère

CLOTHING & ACCESSORIES

Bouvy (1, D6) Conservatively-dressed Bouvy sells reliable, risk-averse fashion for women and men (Armani, Tommy Hilfiger, Parallele), plus made-to-measure suits. The women's collection is accessed off Avenue Louise; the men's from Avenue de la Toison d'Or.
02 513 07 48 www.bouvy.be (French only) Ave Louise 4, Ixelles 11am-6.30pm Mon, 10am-6.30pm Tue-Sat M Louise

Christa Reniers (2, B3) Stunning contemporary jewellery for women and men is made in a workshop on the premises and then left to gleam in the otherwise austere interior. The treasure chest includes bejewelled silver and gold rings, earrings, necklaces and chokers.
02 510 06 60 www.christareniers.com Rue Antoine Dansaert 29, Lower Town 10.30am-1pm & 2-6.30pm Mon-Sat M Ste Catherine Bourse premetro

Christophe Coppens (2, A2) This shop sells artwork for your head, with the millinery running the gamut of stylistic invention from prim, feminine little bowlers to items resembling deluxe pleated shower caps and large, durable pastries. Coppens is a materialistic designer, using silk, felt, straw, wool and more in his creations.
02 512 77 97 Rue Léon Lepage 2, Lower Town 11am-6pm Tue-Sun M Ste Catherine

Delvaux (2, E5) Coveted by leather fetishists worldwide, Delvaux produces museum-piece purses, handbags, carry bags and other accessories, most in stylishly subdued colours that won't clash with everything else in your wardrobe. Even the leather-tagged key rings look snazzy, though at €45 apiece you'd want them to.
02 512 71 98 Galerie de la Reine 31, Lower Town 10am-6.30pm Mon-Sat M Gare Centrale

Les Enfants d'Édouard (Map p33) Judging by the racks of cool, preloved designer-wear inside, Édouard must have some pretty smartly dressed children. Old bomber jackets hang elbow to worn elbow with suits, while discarded

CLOTHING & SHOE SIZES

Women's Clothing

Aust/UK	8	10	12	14	16	18
Europe	36	38	40	42	44	46
Japan	5	7	9	11	13	15
USA	6	8	10	12	14	16

Women's Shoes

Aust/USA	5	6	7	8	9	10
Europe	35	36	37	38	39	40
France only	35	36	38	39	40	42
Japan	22	23	24	25	26	27
UK	3½	4½	5½	6½	7½	8½

Men's Clothing

Aust	92	96	100	104	108	112
Europe	46	48	50	52	54	56
Japan	S	M	M		L	
UK/USA	35	36	37	38	39	40

Men's Shirts (Collar Sizes)

Aust/Japan	38	39	40	41	42	43
Europe	38	39	40	41	42	43
UK/USA	15	15½	16	16½	17	17½

Men's Shoes

Aust/UK	7	8	9	10	11	12
Europe	41	42	43	44½	46	47
Japan	26	27	27.5	28	29	30
USA	7½	8½	9½	10½	11½	12½

Measurements approximate only; try before you buy.

party frocks wait patiently for their next soiree. There are two adjoining shops, one for guys and one for gals.
☎ 02 640 42 45 ✉ **Ave Louise 175, Ixelles** 🕓 **10am-6pm Tue-Sat** **M Louise**

Olivier Strelli (1, E6) The subtle chic of Congo-born Strelli's garments for men and women is on show here, where smart cuts, wintry colours and distinctive textures are the name of the fashion game. There's another branch in St Géry at

Stijl for style

Rue Antoine Dansaert 44.
☎ 02 512 56 07 💻 **www.strelli.be** ✉ **Ave Louise 72, Ixelles** 🕓 **10am-6pm Mon-Sat** **M Louise**

Stijl (2, A2) Twenty years young and still cutting-edge, Stijl is the rallying point in Brussels for the creations of successful Antwerp-based designers such as Dries Van Noten, as well as up-and-coming sartorial talent. It sells contemporary outfits for men, women and children, plus handsome accessories from footwear to neckwear.
☎ 02 512 03 13 ✉ **Rue Antoine Dansaert 74, Lower Town** 🕓 **10.30am-6.30pm Mon-Sat** **M Ste Catherine** **Bourse premetro**

ARTS & ANTIQUES

Broc Ant Art (1, C5) One of Rue Blaes' many *brocante* (bric-a-brac) dealers, this shop reflects the old-world nothing-is-disposable spirit of the Marolles. The array of antiques and collectable junk here has included old backgammon sets, satchels, clocks, Manneken Pis playing cards and the odd bowling ball.
☎ **02 511 43 04** ✉ **Rue Blaes 59, Marolles** 🕓 **10am-6pm Mon-Fri, 10am-3pm Sat** **M Porte de Hal**

Galerie Lorelei (1, D5) It's worth visiting this place to try to decode artworks with a 'fantastic' or contemporary surrealist bent, such as Che Guevara's face painted on a cow or quirky 3-D collages rising up out of a picture frame. Some of the most intriguing works are the ice-bound images of Gaston Bogaert and the cartoon cities of Charles Fazzino.
☎ 02 513 52 19 ✉ **Place du Grand Sablon 3, Sablon** 🕓 **2.30-6.30pm Thu & Fri, 11.30am-1pm & 2.30-6.30pm Sat & Sun** **M Porte de Namur**

Sablon Antiques Center (1, D5) This co-op of 20 antiques dealers is a good place to begin sizing up the Sablon collectables scene. It sells statuettes, vases, jewellery and musical instruments, but you'll have trouble lugging some of the other items out the door – such as the marble-topped bureaus and the Móndial motorbike.
☎ 02 502 19 29 💻 **www.antiquessablon.com** ✉ **Place du Grand Sablon 39, Sablon** 🕓 **10am-6pm** **M Porte de Namur**

Senses Art Nouveau (1, D4) This is a handsome gallery of Art Nouveau-modelled

Sablon Antiques Center

trinkets, from handcrafted Belgian pewter and crystal to champagne stoppers adorned with coloured Murano glass. Some items take their cues from the art world, such as the porcelain cups and saucers inspired by Klimt's *The Kiss*.
☎ 02 502 15 30 💻 **www.senses-artnouveau.com** ✉ **Rue Lebeau 31, Sablon** 🕓 **11am-6.30pm Tue-Sun** **M Gare Centrale**

MUSIC & BOOKS

Anticyclone des Açores (2, E3) This travel specialist has a name like a weather warning and thousands of guidebooks, trekking logs, diving and sailing manuals, phrasebooks, and maps of Brussels, Belgium and places further afield. The knowledgeable staff will help you find what you're looking for. **☎ 02 217 52 46 🖳 www.anticyclonedesacores.com ✉ Rue du Fossé aux Loups 34, Lower Town 🕔 10.30am-6.30pm Mon-Sat Ⓜ De Brouckère 🚊 Bourse premetro**

Bozarshop (1, E4) This fine-arts bookshop has an impressive collection, covering African and European art, Art Nouveau architecture and scribes such as Georges Simenon, plus some classical music CDs. To prove how eclectic the fine-arts world is, it stocks an obvious bestseller called *Extraordinary Chickens*. **☎ 02 507 83 33 ✉ Palais des Beaux-Arts (Bozar),**

Arty books at Bozarshop

Rue Ravenstein 23, Upper Town 🕔 10am-6pm Tue-Sun Ⓜ Parc

Goupil-O-Phone (2, B5) This earthy emporium of new and second-hand music has LPs, CDs and DVDs filed under such styles as funk, pop, jazz, folk, trance and 'Français', with lots of stuff sold at *'prix fou!'* ('crazy price!'). Those who'd rather listen to Radiohead and the White Stripes via a needle than a laser can often find limited-edition 33s of newly released albums. **☎ 02 511 00 74 ✉ Blvd Anspach 101, Lower Town 🕔 10.30am-7pm Ⓜ De Brouckère 🚊 Bourse premetro**

La Boîte à Musique (1, E4) This heavyweight classical music shop has an A to Z of international composers and operas on CD, plus performance videos and DVDs. If someone at home is driving you crazy with rap or boy/girl bands, threaten to give them a classical education with the collected works of Bach: 12 boxes' worth, with 11 to 16 CDs in each box. **☎ 02 513 09 65 🖳 www.pavane.com/bam ✉ Rue Ravenstein 17, Upper Town 🕔 9.30am-4pm Mon-Sat Ⓜ Parc**

La Librairie de Rome (1, D6) This is a comprehensive stockist of English-language magazines, newspapers and books. Get your copy of *Elle*, *Gay Times*, *Golf Digest* or the *Daily Mirror*, then browse the paperbacks in the back room. **☎ 02 511 79 37 ✉ Rue Jean Stats 16a, St Gilles 🕔 8am-8pm Ⓜ Louise**

Sterling Books (2, E3) This shop stocks a sterling range of English-language books, from Zadie Smith to the Hogwarts School of Witchcraft & Wizardry, plus lots of crime paperbacks and pulp fiction for those easy-to-please readers. At the front entrance are several shelves of books on the Belgian capital. **☎ 02 223 62 23 🖳 www.sterling-books.be ✉ Rue du Fossé aux Loups 38, Lower Town 🕔 10am-7pm Mon-Sat, noon-6.30pm Sun Ⓜ De Brouckère**

Villette

Villette is the story of Lucy Snowe, an Englishwoman who finds work in a girls' boarding school in a large European city in the mid-19th century and falls desperately in love with the school's autocratic professor. It's also partly the story of author Charlotte Brontë, who based the novel (published in 1853) on her own experiences teaching in a Brussels school in the early 1840s. The novel's depiction of the city of Villette (aka Brussels) is less than complimentary, a theme captured succinctly by the book's dismissive title, which implies 'little town'. Earlier, Brontë had written *The Professor*, a novel similarly based on her time in Brussels.

COMICS

Brüsel (2, C4) This gallery of comic-strip genius sells the illustrated works of Belgian favourites like Peyo and the more contemporary François Schuiten – a book from his famous *Les Cités Obscures* series (see the boxed text on p13) provided the shop with its name. International comics include Katsuhiro Otomo's *Akira* and *Ghost World* by Daniel Clowes, who also came up with the terrific *David Boring* series.
☎ 02 502 35 52 www.brusel.com (French only) ✉ Blvd Anspach 100, Lower Town 10.30am-6.30pm Mon-Sat, noon-6.30pm Sun M De Brouckère Bourse premetro

Centre Belge de la Bande Dessinée Shop (1, E2) The pictorial subject matter in the bookshop of the marvellous Belgian Centre for Comic Strip Art (p13) ranges from wizardry to animal antics to social commentary – something for everyone, in other words. The shop also sells comic-themed figurines and framed prints.
☎ 02 219 19 80 ✉ Rue des Sables 20, Lower Town 10am-6pm Tue-Sun M Gare Centrale

La Boutique Tintin

La Boutique Tintin (2, E5) Engage your imagination with the adventures of the onion-headed cult cartoon figure with the raggedy white dog. There's a limited selection of English-translated Tintin and Milou (aka Snowy) stories behind the counter; alternatively, you can pick up posters, toys and clothes created in their images.
☎ 02 514 51 52 www.store.tintin.com ✉ Rue de la Colline 13, Lower Town 10am-6pm Mon-Sat, 11am-5pm Sun M Gare Centrale Bourse premetro

Pêle-Mêle (1, C4) This store finds new homes for second-hand editions of Lombard, Dupuis, Casterman and the output of other famous comic-book publishers, though French is the lingua franca of the majority of the publications. It also sells assorted magazines, CDs, DVDs, videos, paperbacks and other books, including material on Brussels.
☎ 02 548 78 00 www.pele-mele.be (French only) ✉ Blvd Maurice Lemonnier 55, Lower Town 10am-6.30pm Mon-Sat M De Brouckère Anneessens premetro

Sales & Marketing

The best place for *brocante* (bric-a-brac) is the Marolles' **Place du Jeu de Balle Flea Market** (1, C6; 7am-2pm), where junk rules supreme and haggling is done firmly but politely. For genuine antiques, attend the **Place du Grand Sablon Antiques Market** (1, D5; 9am-5pm Sat, 9am-1pm Sun). The **Marché du Midi** (1, A6; 6am-1pm Sun) is a huge general market, selling ethnic foods and clothing around the Gare du Midi. The gigantic, annual **Jette Marché** is held early in September around Avenue de Jette. For foodstuffs, try the delightful **Consumables Fair** (Map p33; 2-7pm Wed) on Place du Chatelain in Ixelles.

FOOD & DRINK

AD Anspach (2, C4) There are plenty of well-stocked shelves to ransack in this busy central supermarket, which has serviceable fruit, vegetable and *charcuterie* (delicatessen) sections. Out front is a giant vending machine (sorry, *epicerie automatique*) where you can satisfy your cravings for cigarettes, pâté, yoghurt and orange juice 24 hours a day.
02 512 80 87 Blvd Anspach 63, Lower Town 9am-6pm Mon-Thu, Sat & Sun, 9am-9pm Fri M De Brouckère Bourse premetro

Champigros (2, B3) At this family-run, street-side stall, a specialist supplier of fine fungi to assorted restaurants and wannabe celebrity chefs, you can buy brown shiitake specimens, yellow *girelles*, *blonds des Paris* and many other

Fungi fix: Champigros

seasonal varieties. There are also bottled mushies, garlic and other gourmet ingredients.
02 511 74 98 www.champigros.be (French & Dutch only) Rue Melsens 22, Lower Town 7.30am-5pm Tue-Sat M Ste Catherine

Den Teepot (Bioshop) (1, C3) No artificial flavourings, colourings or preservatives are to be found within a genetically modified mile of Bioshop, which has an abundance of organic juices, pastas and jams, as well as biodynamic fruit, vegetables and bread. So healthy it's sickening.
02 511 94 02 www.bioshop.be (Dutch only) Rue des Chartreux 66, Lower Town 8.30am-7pm Mon-Sat M Ste Catherine Bourse premetro

Tea & Eat (1, D6) A modest anagram but an impressive range of more than 90 teas, costing €4 to €16 per 100g. If you're considering an urban picnic, you can buy wines and fine foodstuffs like gourmet *confiture* (jam). It also runs a teahouse a bit further down the street, specialising in club sandwiches and bagels.
02 513 03 08 www.tea-eat.be (French only) Rue de Stassart 124, Ixelles 10am-8pm Mon-Sat M Louise

FOR CHILDREN

Dandoy (2, D5) This purveyor of delicious traditional biscuits has trays of cinnamon-flavoured *speculoos*, a gum-gluing sweet bread called *cramique* (or *pain au sucre*), and large shards of *biscuit de Dinant*, known to dentists around Brussels as 'teeth-breakers' due to the globs of honey used in the recipe.
02 511 03 26 Rue au Beurre 31, Lower Town 8.30am-6.30pm Mon-Sat M De Brouckère Bourse premetro

La Courte Echelle (2, E6) This enchanting shop has everything your child needs to equip themselves for life in a doll's house, from

Sweet treats at Dandoy

miniature tables to teensy chess sets and plates of sushi. A wonderful microcosm of domestic decoration, it's as if Ikea opened a home-wares outlet in Lilliput, except that the stuff here is preassembled and much of it is made by Belgian artisans.
02 512 47 59 www.lacourteechelle.com (French only) Rue des Eperonniers 12, Lower Town 11.30am-1.30pm & 2-6pm Mon, Tue & Thu-Sat M Gare Centrale Bourse premetro

Tinok (Map p33) Well-heeled families come here to stock up on this season's must-have designer childrenswear and toys (the latest rage is 'Dimpel' bears, apparently), plus colour-coordinated accessories like prams, cots and highchairs. The clothing is designed to be modelled around town by kids up to six years old.
☎ 02 646 35 87 ✉ Ave Louise 165, Ixelles 🕔 10.30am-6.30pm Mon-Sat Ⓜ Louise

CHOCOLATE

Galler (2, D5) This superb *confiserie* (confectioner's shop) sells liqueur pralines and handmade ice cream with names like *blanc absolu* and *noir extrême.* A pack of 64 liqueur-filled depth charges (Kirsch, *framboise, rhum*, Curaçao, *anisette*) costs around €70.
☎ 02 502 02 66 ✉ Rue au Beurre 44, Lower Town 🕔 10am-9pm Ⓜ De Brouckère 🚋 Bourse premetro

Godiva (2, E5) No relation to the lady who rode *au naturel* through the streets of Coventry, but similarly capable of making people swoon when they get a whiff of the chocolate in its Grand Place store. There are branches in the Galeries St Hubert and the Place du Grand Sablon.
☎ 02 511 25 37 💻 www.godiva.be ✉ Grand Place 22, Lower Town 🕔 9am-10pm Mon-Sat Ⓜ De Brouckère 🚋 Bourse premetro

Indulge at Godiva

Neuhaus (2, E5) It must be hell for recovering chocoholics to walk past Neuhaus' glamorous window display in the Galeries St Hubert without succumbing to a smash-and-grab impulse. Gorge yourself on gaily packaged bonbons or slabs of delectable dark chocolate.
☎ 02 512 63 59 💻 www.neuhaus.be ✉ Galerie de la Reine 25-27, Lower Town 🕔 10am-8pm Mon-Sat, 11am-7pm Sun Ⓜ Gare Centrale

Pierre Marcolini (1, D5) This designer-chocolate studio has a huge range of individual sweets and gourmet boxed sets with which to treat yourself. And there's probably also a small cake or tartlet in the front window with your name on it. The beautiful praline packaging is provided by leather specialist Delvaux (p40).
☎ 02 514 12 06 💻 www.marcolini.be ✉ Place du Grand Sablon 39, Sablon 🕔 10am-7pm Mon-Thu, 10am-9pm Fri, 9am-9pm Sat, 9am-7pm Sun Ⓜ Porte de Namur

Planète Chocolat (2, C6) The core of this planet is 100% molten cocoa butter. Watch the choc-moulding demonstrations, order some

Choosing Chocolate

It's an offence under Belgian law to go on a diet in Brussels. Who'd want to anyway, with the sensational range of high-quality (as opposed to just sugary) chocolates on offer here? The most common type of chocolate is the humble praline (filled chocolate), the mainstay of specialist chains like Leonidas and Godiva, and raised to an art form in *confiseries* (confectioner's shops) such as Galler, Wittamer and Pierre Marcolini. Praline variations include *caraque* (plain or dark chocolate), crème fraîche (filling made using whipped cream), *gianduja* (blending of milk chocolate and hazelnut paste) and *nougatine* (with crunchy nuts and toffee).

personalised confectionery, or just sit in the café adjoining this innovative chocolate factory and put your sweet tooth to work.
☎ 02 511 07 55 ✉ **Rue du Lombard 24, Lower Town** ⏲ **10am-6.30pm Mon-Fri, 11am-6.30pm Sat, 11am-5pm Sun** Ⓜ **Gare Centrale** 🚋 **Bourse premetro**

Wittamer (1, D5) All of the delicious goodies on display in this superquality, room-sized chocolate box are made on the premises, including the *fruits confit* (chunks of fruit dipped in confection) and *pate de fruit* (sweet moulded fruit juice). You'll pay €5 for 100g of chocolate truffles.
☎ 02 512 37 42 💻 **www.wittamer.com** ✉ **Place du Grand Sablon 6, Sablon** ⏲ **10am-7pm Wed-Sat, 10am-6pm Sun & Mon** Ⓜ **Porte de Namur**

BEER

Beer Mania (1, F6) Poor souls suffering from an excessive desire for amber fluids can get some comfort from the 400 beers lining the walls here, a statistic proudly announced over the front door. Those whose condition is particularly acute should buy one of the 3L magnums of Duvel (€30).
☎ 02 512 17 88 💻 **www.beermania.be** ✉ **Chaussée de Wavre 174-176, Ixelles** ⏲ **11am-7pm Mon-Sat** Ⓜ **Trône**

De Biertempel (2, E5) True Belgian beer worshippers enter on their knees and often stay there after taking in the 450-plus beers on offer (along with matching glassware) in this shrine to the humble boiled grain. If you don't know where to start, ask the helpful proprietor for direction.
☎ 02 502 19 06 ✉ **Rue du Marché aux Herbes 56, Lower Town** ⏲ **9.30am-7pm** Ⓜ **De Brouckère** 🚋 **Bourse premetro**

Délices et Caprices (2, C5) Another well-stocked beer shop ready to provide a liquid education, this one is just around the corner from Grand Place. It's identifiable by the Mort Subite banner over the entrance and the pot-bellied tourists who can't quite drag themselves away from the front window.
☎ 02 512 14 51 ✉ **Rue des Pierres 51, Lower Town** ⏲ **10am-4.30pm Mon-Fri** Ⓜ **De Brouckère** 🚋 **Bourse premetro**

LACE

F Rubbrecht (2, D5) This well-established shop has a solid range of handsome lace items, from petite drinks coasters to the odd *mouchoir* (handkerchief) and tablecloth. Remember that not all Belgian lace is handmade – much of it is machined into shape – so if you want an authentic handcrafted piece, ask for it.
☎ 02 512 02 18 💻 **www.rubbrecht.com** ✉ **Grand Place 23, Lower Town** ⏲ **10am-6.45pm** Ⓜ **De Brouckère** 🚋 **Bourse premetro**

Lace Palace (2, D6) This place stocks professionally woven lace in the material's three primary colours: white, black and beige. Aside from the usual assortment of lightweight souvenirs, you'll also find unusual lace apparel here. Women's tops cost from €50 and there are also some snug outfits to try to force your kids to wear.
☎ 02 512 56 34 ✉ **Rue de la Violette 1-3, Lower Town** ⏲ **8.30am-late Mon-Sat, 9.30am-late Sun** Ⓜ **Gare Centrale** 🚋 **Bourse premetro**

Manufacture Belge de Dentelles (2, E5) If your concept of lace is limited to the doilies you once saw in Grandma Fudge's Tearoom, visit this shop and gaze at the intricate woven patterns that blanket the walls and shelves. These quality goods speak of extraordinary patience and attention to detail.
☎ 02 511 44 77 ✉ **Galerie de la Reine 6-8, Lower Town** ⏲ **9.30am-6pm Mon-Sat** Ⓜ **Gare Centrale** 🚋 **Bourse premetro**

Eating

Belgian cuisine has the kind of reputation that other cuisines would starve themselves for. It combines an indigenous fussiness in the way food is prepared (fresh is best) with bold innovation, a sense of occasion, generous servings and the French flair for *haute cuisine*. Brussels is a city that savours and delights in its food, from the offerings of traditional eateries to the Turkish, Italian, African, Asian and other cuisines that reflect its international population. Elsewhere, long lunches are a symbol of overindulgence; here, they're a sign of appreciation.

A typical breakfast includes sliced meats, cheese, bread and coffee, while Bruxellois tend to snack on *maatjes* (herring fillets) or a *sandwich garni* (a filled half-baguette). During lunches and dinners, everything from Ardennes boar to horse meat can make an appearance on your plate. The most prevalent dish is *moules et frites* (mussels and chips; see the boxed text on p49), the smell of which dominates the air of crowded restaurant districts like Ilôt Sacré, but other seafood such as *crevettes* (shrimps) and *anguilles* (eels) are popular too, particularly around the old fish market in Ste Catherine. Many meats are marinated in the fine local beers, one delicious example being *lapin à la kriek* (rabbit stewed in cherry beer). Vegetable-wise, there are the superb *truffe* (truffle) and *chicon* (chicory). The poor Brussels sprout, however, is usually relegated to supermarkets, not menus.

Smoking is common in restaurants, cafés and brasseries, though some places ban fuming outright and others allocate a separate (rarely self-enclosed) room for the practice. A service charge is almost always included in restaurant bills, but you can leave a tip if you feel like it. Note that many menus are written exclusively in French and Flemish.

Price Ranges

The prices in this chapter indicate the cost of a two-course meal with one drink for one person.

$	up to €14
$$	€15 to €24
$$$	€25 to €40
$$$$	over €40

Dine like royalty at Belga Queen

EU AREA

The stylish Balthazar

Balthazar (3, B1) $$-$$$
modern European
This is an ultra stylish but unintimidating space for those with a taste for modern European cuisine – scampi-sprinkled risotto is a highly satisfying choice. Dine while surrounded by chic, high-backed chairs and benches in the cool main space, or take your plate out onto the gorgeous, low-walled terrace for some alfresco chomping.
☎ 02 742 06 00 ✉ **Rue Archimède 63** ⏲ **noon-2.30pm & 6.30-10.30pm Mon-Fri, 6-11pm Sat** Ⓜ **Schuman** Ⓥ

Chez Moi (1, F5) $$
modern European
A Mont Blanc pen's throw from the gleaming EU parliamentary enclave, Chez Moi is where self-inflated Eurocrats feign interest in each other's loudly announced opinions on policies, portfolios and sport. The lunch-time plat du jour is usually good value: three courses for around €18.
☎ 02 280 26 66 ✉ **Rue du Luxembourg 66** ⏲ **noon-3pm & 7-11pm Mon-Fri** Ⓜ **Trône**

L'Esprit de Sel (3, B3) $$-$$$
traditional Belgian
This brisk, popular, combination brasserie-restaurant is used to doing business with EU personnel and visiting corporate dignitaries, as evidenced by the English menus. Both of its dining halls have a light, fresh ambience, and the menu throws up hearty treats like terrine of Atlantic fish and stewed leg of lamb.
☎ 02 230 60 40 💻 **www.espritdesel.be** ✉ **Place Jourdan 52-54** ⏲ **noon-midnight** Ⓜ **Schuman** ♿ **fair** 👶

Maison Antoine (3, B3) $
friturie
This quick-service chip shop is an institution in Place Jourdan, where for decades it's been filling paper cones with hot *frites* and topping them with mayonnaise or one of more than 20 other sauces. You can also get a *pain frites* (chip sandwich) and a range of burgers, kebabs and other snacks.
☎ 02 230 54 56 ✉ **Place Jourdan 1** ⏲ **11.30am-1am Sun-Thu, 11.30am-2am Fri & Sat** Ⓜ **Schuman** ♿ **good** 👶

Maison Antoine

Rosticceria Fiorentina (3, B1) $$
Italian
At this unabashedly Italian trattoria, where paper tablecloths are considered far more respectable than linen, the mains are so hearty you'll need an extra stomach to fit them in. Office workers come here to tuck into Tuscan treats at lunch time and leave having peppered their clothes with pasta sauce.
☎ 02 734 92 36 ✉ **Rue Archimède 43** ⏲ **noon-2.30pm & 6.30-9.30pm Mon-Fri, 6.30-9.30pm Sun** Ⓜ **Schuman** 👶 Ⓥ

Sushi Factory (3, B1) $-$$
Japanese
This small corner sushi store in the heart (or stomach) of EU territory doles out prepackaged sushi to Euro-minions who don't have time to stop and smell the *wasabi*. Those who do have time perch themselves on stools and contemplate one of the Japanese 'banquet' lunch options.
☎ 02 230 74 32 ✉ **Blvd Charlemagne 44** ⏲ **11am-8pm Mon-Fri** Ⓜ **Schuman**

GRAND PLACE AREA & ILÔT SACRÉ

Al Barmaki (2, D6) **$$**
Lebanese
This expansive, breezy-blue, casual Lebanese restaurant does a vigorous trade in falafel, kebabs and superior meze. It's a great, centrally located place to fuel up after a day of exploration in the vicinity of Grand Place.
☎ 02 513 08 34 ✉ Rue des Eperonniers 65 ⏲ 7pm-midnight Mon-Sat Ⓜ Gare Centrale 🚼 Ⓥ

Aux Armes de Bruxelles (2, E4) **$$$**
traditional Belgian
Locals are constantly darting in and out of this highly regarded restaurant, one of the few Rue des Bouchers places where you'll get exactly what you pay for. Flag down a waiter and order some turbot (European flatfish) or a steaming pot of *moules*.
☎ 02 511 55 50 💻 www.armesdebruxelles.be ✉ Rue des Bouchers 13 ⏲ noon-11pm Tue-Sun Ⓜ De Brouckère 🚋 Bourse premetro

Belga Queen (2, E2) **$$$-$$$$**
modern Belgian
This is the trendsetting monarch of the city's chic restaurant scene. Its grand central hall is usually filled with a stylish young crowd nibbling at lobster limbs or something else from the seafood-heavy menu. There's a sleek *ecailler* (oyster bar) near the front entrance.
☎ 02 217 21 87 💻 www.resto.be/belgaqueen ✉ Rue du Fossé aux Loups 32 ⏲ noon-2.30pm & 7pm-midnight Ⓜ De Brouckère Ⓥ

Moules et Frites

The country's national dish is without doubt mussels and chips. The mussels, mostly from the Netherlands, are usually cooked in white wine and accompanied by a landslide of chips. The local rule of thumb is to eat mussels only during months with an 'r' in their name and to avoid eating any that haven't opened properly once cooked. When bought from one of Belgium's ubiquitous *frituries* (chip shops), chips are served in paper cones and obliterated by mayonnaise (or other sauces); to assist you in this gourmet meal, a tiny plastic fork will be poked into the topmost chip.

Café Métropole (2, E2) **$-$$**
café
At this stalwart of the grand café scene, waiters plough through the magnificent interior with the imperturbable air of cruise liners, and grey-haired citizens sit at outside tables arranged like cinema seats to face the busy boulevard. This place is so formal, even the iced tea comes in brandy balloons.
☎ 02 219 23 84 ✉ Place de Brouckère 31 ⏲ 9am-1am Sun-Thu, 9am-2am Fri & Sat Ⓜ De Brouckère ♿ good

Chez Léon (2, E4) **$-$$**
traditional Belgian
The house speciality at this large, perpetually crowded, long-serving eatery is *moules et frites*. You can get this pair of Belgian delicacies, plus a beer, for €12. To up the ante to a hefty, pungent 1kg pot of mussels costs €10 extra. There's another branch at Bruparck (p31).
☎ 02 513 04 26 💻 www.chezleon.be ✉ Rue des Bouchers 18 ⏲ noon-11pm Ⓜ De Brouckère 🚋 Bourse premetro ♿ fair 🚼

Hémisphère (2, F4) **$**
café
Sup in soft-cushioned style in the midst of Hémisphère's silky, lantern-hung interior, a cheerful medley of Far Eastern décor. The internationally flavoured food is lovely (try the couscous studded with chicken and vegetables) and the staff are easy-going.
☎ 02 513 93 70 ✉ Rue de l'Écuyer 65 ⏲ noon-3pm & 7-11.30pm Mon-Fri, 7pm-late Sat Ⓜ De Brouckère ♿ fair 🚼 Ⓥ

La Maison du Cygne (2, D5) **$$$$**
French, modern Belgian
Two restaurants occupy the 17th-century building called Le Cygne (The Swan): L'Ommegang, a brasserie

Caveat Emptor

Brussels' highest concentration of restaurants is arguably wedged into the culinary crawlspace just off Grand Place called Rue des Bouchers. But, unfortunately, in this case quantity doesn't mean quality. Most of the eateries trade expensively off the street's reputation and do little to live up to it – overpriced and underflavoured meals are as common as *moules*. There are a few places, however, that offer a decent (and in some cases exceptional) dining experience. Try Aux Armes de Bruxelles (p49), Chez Léon (p49), Saint Laurent (at right) or Taverne du Passage (below).

accessed from Grand Place, and, upstairs, La Maison du Cygne, an exceptional Belgo-French restaurant entered from Rue Charles Buls. Book a table with views over the square at the latter and give your senses a grandiose treat.
☎ **02 511 82 44** 💻 **www.lamaisonducygne.be** ✉ **Rue Charles Buls 2** 🕐 **noon-2pm & 7-10pm Mon-Fri, 7-10pm Sat** Ⓜ **De Brouckère** 🚊 **Bourse premetro**

Le Roy d'Espagne (2, D5) **$$-$$$**
traditional Belgian
Ensconced in the decorative Maison des Boulangers, the former bakers' guildhall, this atmospheric café-pub serves traditional Belgian treats like *stoemp*, a Bruxellois hotpot with sausages, bacon, potatoes and other vegetables, and *lapin à la kriek*. Mind the horse when you're making for an upstairs table.
☎ **02 513 08 07** 💻 **www.roydespagne.be** ✉ **Grand Place 1** 🕐 **10am-1am** Ⓜ **De Brouckère** 🚊 **Bourse premetro** 👶

L'Intermezzo (2, E3) **$**
Italian
You'd expect an Italian restaurant located opposite an opera house to have a melodramatic air, but L'Intermezzo has opted for a relaxed, modern style that attracts young and old alike. Try the delicious *lasagnette* (ribbons of lasagne coated in gorgonzola) or something else from the dependable blackboard menu.
☎ **02 218 03 11** ✉ **Rue des Princes 16** 🕐 **noon-3pm Mon-Thu, noon-3pm & 7-10pm Fri & Sat** Ⓜ **De Brouckère** Ⓥ

Mykonos (2, E6) **$**
Middle Eastern
It's hard to distinguish between the myriad pitta and kebab places crowding Rue du Marché aux Fromages with their outdoor tables. But Mykonos is worth trying, as it's smack in the middle of this entertaining food street and has a great range of stuffed pocket bread.
☎ **02 513 73 54** ✉ **Rue du Marché aux Fromages 8** 🕐 **11am-6am** Ⓜ **Gare Centrale** 👶 Ⓥ

Saint Laurent (2, E4) **$$$**
traditional Belgian
This elegant, glass-roofed eatery is often dismissed in favour of more rustic restaurants on Rue des Bouchers by budget-conscious tourists, but menu prices compare favourably with nearby places. Comfortable booths make a nice change from the usual hard-backed chairs, and specialities such as herb-basted eel are worth trying.
☎ **02 502 46 02** 💻 **www.saintlaurent.be (French & Dutch only)** ✉ **Rue des Bouchers 5** 🕐 **11.30am-midnight** Ⓜ **De Brouckère** 🚊 **Bourse premetro**

Sea Grill (2, F3) **$$$$**
seafood
Before dining on some of Brussels' (if not Belgium's) freshest, most expertly cooked seafood in a room decorated with glass-etched Norwegian fjords, sip an apéritif under the arch of the Romanesque 12th-century wall that's been incorporated into Sea Grill's rock pool-decorated forecourt.
☎ **02 227 31 20** 💻 **www.resto.be/seagrill** ✉ **Radisson SAS Hotel, Rue du Fossé aux Loups 47** 🕐 **noon-2pm & 7-11pm Mon-Fri, 7pm-midnight Sat** Ⓜ **De Brouckère** ♿ **fair**

Taverne du Passage (2, E4) **$$-$$$**
traditional Belgian, French
Mussels, *crevettes* and other meat-flavoured meals are served up in this dignified 1920s eatery, where local businesspeople and tourists are greeted by no-nonsense

waiters and an excellent wine list. For something simple but tasty, try the vol-au-vents with *volaille* (poultry).
☎ 02 512 37 31 💻 www.tavernedupassage.com ✉ Galerie de la Reine 30 🕐 noon-midnight Ⓜ Gare Centrale 👶

Waka Moon (2, E6) $$
African
This cosy corner café dishes out tasty African cooking to the loyal clientele who perch themselves at perilously sloping outside tables or on zebra-patterned chairs in the low-lit interior. If you get the chance, try the grilled fillet of *tilopia* (a tropical fish) in lemon-and-onion sauce.
☎ 02 502 10 32 ✉ Rue des Eperonniers 60 🕐 11.30am-3pm & 7-11pm Mon-Fri, 7-11pm Sat Ⓜ Gare Centrale

IXELLES & ST GILLES

Havana Corner (1, D6) $$
café
Watch the shopped-out lunch crowds mill down pedestrianised Rue Jourdan while enjoying big, stately burgers and other filling (though invariably meaty) café fare. There's also a cocktail-friendly cigar bar on the first floor with live music on Friday and Saturday nights.
☎ 02 534 09 99 ✉ Rue Jourdan 24 🕐 11.30am-9.30pm Mon-Sat Ⓜ Louise ♿ fair

L'Amadeus (Map p33) $$$
international
Vines cover the adjacent buildings and candlelight shadows the tables, enhancing this restaurant's private, do-not-disturb-while-eating allure. The menu is a carnivore's delight (Argentine beef fillet, lamb cutlets and fried Zeebrugge sole) and the wine list is lengthy. Speaking of which, the popular wine bar is open Thursday to Sunday nights.
☎ 02 538 34 27 💻 www.resto.be/amadeus ✉ Rue Veydt 13 🕐 6.30pm-1.30am Tue-Sun, plus 10am-3pm Sun Ⓜ Louise 🚋 No 91

La Quincaillerie (Map p33) $$$
seafood, modern Belgian
The magnificently unusual interior of this one-time metal-wares shop has a touch of Willy Wonka about it, with waiters bustling along metal gangways and an enormous antique clock presiding over proceedings. The atmosphere and excellent brasserie-style meals combine to make it a hugely popular haunt of businesspeople and local suburbanites.
☎ 02 533 98 33 💻 www.quincaillerie.be ✉ Rue du Page 45 🕐 noon-2.30pm & 7pm-midnight Mon-Fri, 7pm-midnight Sat & Sun Ⓜ Porte de Hal 🚋 Horta premetro ♿ good Ⓥ

La Tsampa (Map p33) $-$$
vegetarian
Vegetarians can rejoice over simple, Asian-style food and hearty broths in this homely restaurant. After downing miso soup or *steak de seitan avec champignons* (seitan steak with mushrooms), you can buy untainted bread, vegetables or freshly baked cheesecake in the organic-produce shop out front.
☎ 02 647 03 67 ✉ Rue de Livourne 109 🕐 noon-2pm & 7-9.30pm Mon-Fri Ⓜ Louise, then tram No 93 👶 Ⓥ

The unusual interior of La Quincaillerie

Corporate Cuisine

The following are just a few of the restaurants in Brussels that are well versed in the needs of corporate diners, be they frenetic lunch-time briefings or impression-making dinners. Collective hallmarks of these places include efficient service, attention to culinary detail, dependable wine lists and often set lunches for those whose limited time needs to be spent browsing contracts rather than long menus.

- L'Esprit de Sel (p48) – EU-centric cookery
- Aux Armes de Bruxelles (p49) – local business-brokers
- Belga Queen (p49) – dressed to impress
- La Grande Écluse (p54) – brassy brasserie
- Le Khnopff (below) – symbolically superior
- Tour d'y Voir (p55) – Sablon style
- Le Manufacture (p55) – industrious interior
- Le Vistro (p56) – seafood retreat

Get down to business at La Grande Écluse

Le Khnopff (Map p33) $$$
modern Belgian
Formerly the townhouse where symbolist painter Fernand Khnopff lived and worked from 1888 to 1900, this is now a swish, multilevel restaurant-bar glimpsed from the outside through long burgundy drapes. Business-minded people work out their differences over lime-brushed swordfish and numerous glasses of fine wine.
☎ 02 534 20 04 ✉ Rue St Bernard 1 ⏲ 11.30am-2am Mon-Sat Ⓜ Louise Ⓥ

Les Jardins de Bagatelle (1, E6) $$-$$$
world food
This is literally 'the Garden of Trifles', where cares are washed away by the soporific ambience of the back garden or the colourful salon, not to mention the international wine list. The food is a heavenly mix of global cuisines, including Tibetan *momo* (dumplings), Thai soup and Senegalese chicken, with vegetarians well looked after.
☎ 02 512 12 76 💻 www.jardinsdebagatelle.com ✉ Rue de Berger 12 ⏲ noon-2.30pm & 7-11pm Tue-Fri, 7-11pm Sat Ⓜ Porte de Namur ♿ good 🚼 Ⓥ

L'Estran (1, F6) $$-$$$
seafood
This nautical restaurant loitering discreetly just off lively Place Fernand Cocq is all at sea with its cooking, and much appreciated for it. The menu (which includes English translations) has featured crabs stuffed the Seychellian way and marinated swordfish with coconut milk. Three-course luncheons cost less than €25.
☎ 02 513 57 08 ✉ Rue du Collège 22 ⏲ 11.30am-2pm & 7-10pm Tue-Fri, 7-10pm Sat, 11.30am-2pm Sun Ⓜ Porte de Namur

L'Ultime Atome (1, E6) $$
café
This is a large, gregarious café with few embellishments beyond its honey-coloured walls and overflowing footpath tables. It draws locals (and their kids) like a magnet, and boasts a decent blackboard menu and mighty lists of beer and wine.
☎ 02 511 13 67 ✉ Rue St Boniface 14 ⏲ 11am-12.30am Ⓜ Porte de Namur 🚼 Ⓥ

MAROLLES

Bazaar (1, C6) $$
international
Depending on your mood, the décor of this combined world-food banquet hall and downstairs bar/club (p64) is either entertainingly eccentric or self-consciously over-the-top. The food, a satisfying mix of Moroccan and modern European, is more straightforward than the candles, drapes and Oriental odds 'n' ends strewn around this one-time monastery.
☎ 02 511 26 00
✉ Rue des Capucins 63
🕑 7.30-11.30pm Tue-Sat
M Porte de Hal V

Brasserie la Clef d'Or (1, C6) $
traditional Belgian
Cap off a leisurely rummage through the Marolles flea market (p43) with croquettes, the *potage* (soup) of the day or another of the light meals available at this down-to-earth brasserie. This early-opening place is almost always crowded with jovial, yabbering Bruxellois.
☎ 02 511 97 62 ✉ Place du Jeu de Balle 1 🕑 6am-4pm M Porte de Hal

Comme Chez Soi (1, C4) $$$$
French, modern Belgian
Chef Pierre Wynants' home cooking is considered by many gourmands to be the finest in Brussels. For €90 you can savour a fillet of beef with prized black truffles, while €135 will buy you 50g of Iranian caviar.
☎ 02 512 29 21 🖳 www.commechezsoi.be
✉ Place Rouppe 23
🕑 noon-1.30pm & 7-9.30pm Tue-Sat M Gare du Midi 🚋 Anneessens premetro V

Havana (1, C5) $$-$$$
international
This Latin-flavoured place draws networking expats to its airy, vivid interior to devour *quesadillas*, Finnish meatballs and flambéed scampi, plus vegetarian mains like red pepper and goat's cheese wraps. After dining, you can light up a fat Cuban in one of its three bars.
☎ 02 502 12 24 🖳 www.havana-brussels.com
✉ Rue de l'Epée 4
🕑 7pm-2am Tue, 7pm-3am Wed, 7pm-4am Thu, 7pm-7am Fri & Sat
M Louise V

Ici-même (1, C6) $$
French
The mellow interior, particularly the cosy back lounge, is a comfortable spot to mix-and-match the relatively inexpensive hot and cold dishes on offer. Or you can sit at a table outside and watch the area's intriguing comings and goings over a five-piece dessert plate (€9).
☎ 02 502 54 24 ✉ Rue Haute 204 🕑 noon-2.30pm & 6.30-11pm Tue-Thu, noon-2.30pm & 6.30pm-midnight Fri & Sat M Porte de Hal
♿ good 👶 V

La Gourmandin (1, C5) $$$
French, modern Belgian
This two-storey intimate affair manages to look both chic and rustic at the same time. It's set up on the site of an old butcher's shop and has a small, choosy menu of modern dishes such as *terrine de lapereau* (rabbit terrine) and *crevette*-laced ravioli.
☎ 02 512 98 92 🖳 www.resto.be/gourmandin

Worth a Trip

The city centre is not, of course, the exclusive domain of decent dining in Brussels. There are many other reputable, if not downright stupendous, establishments that lie well beyond the Petit Ring. They include:

- **La Cite du Dragon** (Chinese; ☎ 02 375 80 80; Chaussée de Waterloo 1022, Uccle)
- **La Truffe Noir** (Truffles; ☎ 02 640 44 22; Blvd de la Cambre 12, Ixelles)
- **La Villa Lorraine** (Belgian/French; ☎ 02 374 31 63; Chaussée de la Hulpe 28, Boitsfort)
- **Pantalone** (Italian; ☎ 02 524 13 67; Chaussée de Ninove 690, Anderlecht)
- **Restaurant Bruneau** (Belgian/French; ☎ 02 427 69 78; Ave Broustin 75, Koekelberg)

(French & Dutch only)
✉ Rue Haute 152
🕐 noon-2.30pm & 7-10pm Tue-Fri, 7-10pm Sat, noon-2.30pm Sun & Mon
Ⓜ Porte de Hal ♿ good

La Grande Écluse (1, B5) $$$
French, modern Belgian
The name of this recommended restaurant ('Great Lock') refers to the lock that until 1930 helped regulate the flow of the now-diverted River Senne. The converted site has tables on metal gangways and an attractive terrace, and the excellent modern menu pleases both meat-eaters and vegetarians.
☎ 02 522 30 💻 www.grouptorus.com/Pages/Ecluse/ecluse_histo.html
✉ Blvd Poincaré 77
🕐 noon-2.30pm Mon, noon-2.30pm & 7-10.30pm Tue-Fri, 7-10.30pm Sat
Ⓜ Gare du Midi 🚊 Lemonnier premetro Ⓥ

La Grande Porte (1, C5) $$
traditional Belgian
This is a cheery old café tucked away near the railway line, with paper lanterns hanging from the ceiling and an extension that eschews dark wood for white modernity. The fine traditional Belgian cuisine includes *ballekes aux Mariolennes* (Marolles meatballs) and *chicons aux gratin* (chicory with melted cheese).
☎ 02 512 89 98
✉ Rue Notre-Seigneur 9
🕐 noon-3pm & 6pm-2am Mon-Fri, 6pm-2am Sat Ⓜ Porte de Hal

Le Grand Restaurant (1, D5) $$-$$$
modern Belgian
Sheltering behind the Église des Minimes is this stylish modern brasserie. The outside terrace is shaded from the afternoon sun (assuming the sun isn't already blocked by Belgium's ubiquitous clouds) and attracts a late-lunching crowd. Linguine, grilled meat and salads are some of the menu's staples.
☎ 02 513 13 42 ✉ Rue des Minimes 60 🕐 noon-2.30pm & 7pm-midnight Tue-Fri, noon-midnight Sat & Sun Ⓜ Louise ♿ fair

L'Étoile d'Or (1, B4) $$
traditional Belgian
Also charmingly called De Rotte Planchei (The Rotten Wooden Floor), this humble café sits at the northern end of the Marolles in a warren of tight, quiet, residential streets. Locals descend on this place (particularly at weekends) to devour fine traditional cookery such as *waterzooi*, a creamy meat and vegetable stew.
☎ 02 502 60 48 ✉ Rue des Foulons 30 🕐 noon-2.30pm & 7-10.30pm Mon-Fri, 7-10.30pm Sat Ⓜ Gare du Midi 🚊 Anneessens premetro

SABLON

Canne à Sucre (1, D5) $$$
Caribbean, seafood
This place sparkles with Caribbean verve, from the thatch-worked front window display to the Creole seafood cooking and the spirit-lifting rum cocktails. The fillet of duck with bananas makes a good rum chaser, as do the fresh crabs.
☎ 02 513 03 72
✉ Rue des Pigeons 12
🕐 7.30pm-midnight Mon-Thu, 7.30pm-1.30am Fri & Sat
Ⓜ Porte de Namur

La Pirogue (1, D5) $$
African
Larger than an actual pirogue and presumably a bit more comfortable, this Senegalese food parlour has a small terrace out back and serves up dishes like *yassa* (chicken and onions in a lime sauce), braised *chèvre* (goat) and marinated lamb. African beer is also on the menu.
☎ 02 511 35 25 ✉ Rue Ste Anne 18 🕐 noon-3pm & 6pm-midnight Tue-Fri, noon-3pm & 6pm-1am Sat & Sun
Ⓜ Porte de Namur

African fare: La Pirogue

Le Grain de Sable (1, D5) $$
international
Weekday lunch times see business types eating around the uncluttered, informal bar space or comparing notes and mobile phone

upgrades across a footpath table. The cuisine is reliably tasty, if unadventurous: try the pike perch on a bed of mushroom, aubergine and spinach. Vegetarian meals are often pasta-based.
☎ 02 514 05 83 ✉ Place du Grand Sablon 15-16 ⏲ noon-3pm & 7-11pm Mon-Fri, noon-11pm Sat & Sun Ⓜ Porte de Namur ♿ good Ⓥ

Le Perroquet (1, D5) $-$$
café
This is a laid-back purveyor of creative, inexpensive pittas and salads in an area full of up-market eateries. It's blessed with engaging Art Nouveau décor, a chatty clientele and a lengthy wine list. While you're digesting, check out some of the lovely surrounding buildings in this aristocratic old quarter.
☎ 02 512 99 22 ✉ Rue Watteeu 31 ⏲ 10.30am-midnight Ⓜ Louise Ⓥ

L'Objet de Mon Affection (1, D5) $$
modern Belgian
This is one of the best places on this restaurant-crowded pedestrian *rue*, a stylish den of degustation with a red-rimmed main room, an outside marquee and a smaller chamber near the bar with a few more private tables. The paella Valenciana (with chorizo, chicken and seafood) is a winner.
☎ 02 502 77 83 ✉ Rue de Rollebeek 11 ⏲ 11am-3pm & 6-11pm Ⓜ Gare Centrale Ⓥ

Tour d'y Voir (1, D5) $$-$$$
French, modern Belgian
This place has high ceilings, brick walls, a signature steel-and-brass tower hanging above the front entrance and a reputation for fine modern cooking. Busy businesspeople favour the *lunch rapide*, three courses served in 45 minutes for less than €20, while the *menu prestige* provides five to six courses for around €50.
☎ 02 511 40 43 🖳 www.tourdyvoir.com ✉ 1st fl, Place du Grand Sablon 8/9 ⏲ noon-2pm & 7-11pm Tue-Thu & Sun, noon-2pm & 7pm-midnight Fri & Sat Ⓜ Porte de Namur

Wittamer (1, D5) $-$$
café
The café part of Wittamer's combination patisserie, *glacerie* (ice creamery) and *traiteur* (caterer) on Sablon's central square has a menu of good though overpriced light meals, including quiche, beef *carpaccio* and tomato and *crevette* croquettes. Chocolate and ice cream are prime choices for dessert.
☎ 02 512 37 42 🖳 www.wittamer.com ✉ Place du Grand Sablon 12-13 ⏲ 9.30am-6pm Ⓜ Porte de Namur ♿ fair 🚼 Ⓥ

STE CATHERINE

Jacques (2, B1) $$$
seafood
You can order several *viande* (meat) dishes here, but this well-patronised old salt of the Ste Catherine scene has found its real forte in concocting uncomplicated, outstanding seafood dishes. Straight from the briny to your plate come fresh mussels, oysters, *anguilles*, sole and turbot.
☎ 02 513 27 62 ✉ Quai aux Briques 44 ⏲ noon-2.30pm & 6.30-10.30pm Mon-Sat Ⓜ Ste Catherine

Le Jardin de Catherine (2, B2) $$$
seafood
The courtyard of this seafood connoisseur is a great place for a leisurely lunch on a bright day; alternatively, try the rosewood interior. If you can't decide between fish soup or grilled lobster with *escargots*, take the set menu: three courses for around €40.
☎ 02 513 19 92 🖳 www.jardindecatherine.be ✉ Place Ste Catherine 5 ⏲ noon-2.30pm & 7-11pm Sun-Fri, 7-11pm Sat Ⓜ Ste Catherine

Le Manufacture (1, B3) $$-$$$
French, international
Formerly a Delvaux workshop, Le Manufacture is a big hit with those who like their power lunches accompanied by industrial-strength style. Business suits usually pack the factory-cum-jailhouse interior to sample a weekly-changing menu that has included beef soaked in *kriek*, mustard-swabbed pork kebabs and chorizo 'cake'.
☎ 02 502 25 25 🖳 www.manufacture.be (French only) ✉ Rue Notre-Dame

Sweet Treats

If you're tired of topping up your main course with chocolates, gateau or *crème glacée* (ice cream), head to a bakery or speciality shop like Dandoy (p44) to scoop up some thin and crispy *speculoos* biscuits or other baked goods. Another option you'll find in food stalls is *oliebollen* (literally 'oily balls', a type of doughnut). Speaking of streetside fare, you have to try *gaufres*, Belgian waffles cooked as you wait. And don't worry if someone suggests smothering them in *slagroom* – it's the Flemish word for whipped cream.

du Sommeil 12 noon-2pm & 7-11pm Mon-Fri, 7pm-midnight Sat M Ste Catherine V

Le Paon Royal (2, A3) $$
traditional Belgian
The old-fashioned Royal Peacock has 80 years' experience in plying the denizens of Ste Catherine with traditional Belgian cuisine, such as its delicious *filet Américain* (raw, seasoned minced beef). The well-shaded terrace across the road is good for a late-afternoon beer; more than 50 varieties are available.
☎ 02 513 08 68 www.paonroyal.com (French & Dutch only) ✉ Rue Vieux Marché aux Grains 6 8am-10pm Tue-Thu, 8am-11.30pm Fri & Sat M Ste Catherine

Le Vistro (2, B2) $$$
seafood
This is a diminutive, relaxed seafood eatery with a popular alfresco dining wing set up on the cobblestones of Vismet opposite. Order from an admirable list of ocean-dwelling edibles or take the Bruxellois approach and try the *grand moules* (€20).
☎ 02 512 41 81 www.resto.be/levistro ✉ Quai aux Briques 16 12.30-2.30pm & from 6.30pm M Ste Catherine fair

Strofilia (1, C2) $$
Greek
This Greek restaurant offers tasty salads, meaty mains and, in keeping with its status as a *mezedopolio*, lots of mezes such as *saganaki* (fried cheese), pork balls and grilled red capsicum. It doubles as a wine bar in an attempt to reprise the building's role as a wine warehouse in the 17th century.
☎ 02 512 32 93 www.resto.be/strofilia ✉ Rue du Marché aux Porcs 11 noon-2pm & 7pm-midnight Mon-Fri, 7pm-midnight Sat M Ste Catherine V

ST GÉRY

Arteaspoon (2, A4) $
café
This cosy, minimally decorated café is popular with conversant locals who like their gourmet sandwiches, soups and omelettes accompanied by the strains of modern jazz and artsy reading material. The coffee is better than the average Brussels cuppa and the cheesecake is a crowd-pleaser.
☎ 02 513 51 17 http://arteaspoon.tripod.com (French only) ✉ Rue des Chartreux 32 11.30am-3.30pm Mon & Tue, 11.30am-6pm Wed-Fri, noon-7pm Sat M Ste Catherine Bourse premetro V

Bonsoir Clara (2, B3) $$$
French, international
Deep twin dining rooms, spot-lit zinc-topped tables, a colourful quilt of squares on the wall, and a well-dressed, softly spoken clientele conspire to give Bonsoir Clara a simple, fashionably unruffled air. The seasonal menu rarely disappoints; ditto the impressive wine list.
☎ 02 502 09 90 ✉ Rue Antoine Dansaert 22 noon-2.30pm & 7-11.30pm Mon-Thu, noon-2.30pm & 7pm-midnight Fri, 7-11.30pm Sat & Sun M Ste Catherine Bourse premetro V

Da Kao (2, B3) $-$$
Vietnamese
Inexpensive and filling Vietnamese food is munched in this pastel-swamped restaurant by a dizzying mixture

of shop and office workers, students, families and tourists. If you're feeling audacious, order the curried eels and frog legs, or, if you're just plain hungry, try the special mixed plate (€10).
02 512 67 16 Rue Antoine Dansaert 38 noon-3pm & 6pm-midnight Mon-Fri, noon-midnight Sat & Sun M Ste Catherine Bourse premetro

Den Teepot (1, C3) $
vegetarian
This is one of Brussels' few certifiably authentic vegetarian eateries, complete with farmhouse-kitchen décor, a mixed crowd of legume-lovers and a noticeable lack of cigarette smoke. The plat du jour is great value at under €8, while hearty soups are available for around €2.50.
02 511 94 02 www.bioshop.be (Dutch only) 1st fl, Rue des Chartreux 66 noon-2pm Mon-Sat M Ste Catherine Bourse premetro V

Try classic Belgian dishes at In 't Spinnekopke

In 't Spinnekopke (1, B3) $$-$$$
traditional Belgian
If the ceremonious waiters, 1762 facade or history-crammed interior aren't enough to convince you that this place takes its Flemish traditions seriously, then just try one of the classic beer-soaked Belgian mains such as *pintadeau à la bière de framboise* (guinea-fowl in raspberry beer). There is some tranquil outdoor seating in the square.
02 511 86 95 www.spinnekopke.be Place du Jardin aux Fleurs 1 11am-11pm Mon-Fri, 6pm-midnight Sat M Ste Catherine Bourse premetro

Kasbah (2, B3) $$
Middle Eastern
With apologies to the Clash, the Kasbah rocks. Dozens of softly glowing lanterns float above the heads of diners as they settle onto cushioned benches and chairs to sweep meze into their mouths, or to spoon aromatic stews onto mounds of steaming couscous.
02 502 40 26 Rue Antoine Dansaert 20 noon-3pm & 6.30pm-midnight M Ste Catherine Bourse premetro V

Le Bar à Tapas (2, B5) $-$$
Spanish
Salsa-coloured walls, friendly service, old barrels plugged into the brickwork and large windows opened up to let the street noise in – just some of the hallmarks of this Spanish diner. Evening crowds lap up the good-value tapas and the atmosphere in the heart of St Géry.
02 502 66 02 Borgval 11 noon-12.30am Mon-Fri, 6pm-late Sat & Sun M De Brouckère Bourse premetro V

Le Pain Quotidien (2, B3) $
bakery
This is a no-fuss, scantily decorated *boulangerie* (bakery, this one part of a Belgium-wide chain) where you can order a dirt-cheap *pannet au chocolate et une caffe* (chocolate bread and coffee) for breakfast, or perhaps a savoury pie or sandwich, and scoff it in a

Vegetarian Food

The common view is that modern Belgian cuisine's exceptional reputation implies a strong range of vegetarian meals, not just salads, omelettes and boiled vegetables. But our experience is that vegetarians don't always have it easy in Brussels. The problem is not with the best restaurants, which mostly have great veggie offerings (though not necessarily many choices), but with mid-range Belgian eateries that make a minimal effort with plant food beyond the aforementioned dishes, nonmeat lasagne and fried cheese. Heartily recommended vegetarian meal providers include Den Teepot (above), La Tsampa (p51) and Les Jardins de Bagatelle (p52).

smoke-free environment.
☎ 02 502 23 61 🖳 www.painquotidien.com ✉ Rue Antoine Dansaert 16 🕑 7.30am-6pm Ⓜ Ste Catherine 🚊 Bourse premetro 🚼 ⊠

Totem (2, A5) $$
international, vegetarian
This is a nonconformist, two-in-one corner restaurant, with a 'classic' modish eatery dominated by enormous phantasmagorical artworks and a separate light-and-easy vegetarian restaurant that banishes both smoke and alcohol. Neither place accepts credit cards. While you're here, walk further down narrow Rue de l'Eclipse, so-named because of its unwillingness to admit much sunlight.
☎ 0476 208 609, vegetarian restaurant 0476 552 763 🖳 www.urbanstarnavigator.com ✉ Rue de la Grande Île 42; vegetarian restaurant: Rue de l'Eclipse 13 🕑 8-10.30pm Wed-Sun Ⓜ De Brouckère 🚊 Bourse premetro ♿ fair 🚼 Ⓥ

ST JOSSE & SCHAERBEEK

De Ultieme Hallucinatie (1, F1) $$-$$$
traditional Belgian
This is a classic Art Nouveau eatery with an ornate, dimly lit restaurant in the main house and a back-annexe café. The restaurant's French-slanted food is as rich as its interior, while the café's standard menu includes pasta, fish and omelettes. The only hint of hallucination is the curious ravine effect along one wall of the café.
☎ 02 217 06 14 ✉ Rue Royale 316 🕑 11am-late Mon-Fri, 4pm-late Sat Ⓜ Botanique

L'Ane Vert (1, F1) $$
traditional Belgian
This warm brasserie has an affable home-grown character of its own, epitomised by its choice of name: the Green Donkey. The menu has several vegetarian choices, there's a good drinks list, and the small grouping of outside tables is almost always busy.
☎ 02 217 26 17 🖳 www.anevert.com (French only) ✉ Rue Royale Ste Marie 11 🕑 noon-midnight Mon-Fri, 5pm-midnight Sat Ⓜ Botanique Ⓥ

Metin (1, F1) $
Turkish
This is one of the city's original *pide* establishments, which started inviting people in for Turkish pizza 25 years ago and is still nourishing St Josse locals and curious blow-ins. You can get almost any topping imaginable here, including scampi, gruyere and the contents of a decent-sized vegetable garden.
☎ 02 217 68 63 ✉ Chaussée de Haecht 94 🕑 11am-11pm Wed-Mon Ⓜ Botanique Ⓥ

Palais des Délices $
patisserie
This aptly named Moroccan patisserie palace, with golden walls, tile-topped tables and metal-twisted chairs, has vast trays of cream horns, almond rings, baklava, pistachio logs and date-and-nutmeg parcels.
☎ 02 280 48 40 ✉ Place St Josse 13 🕑 9am-10pm Mon-Sat, noon-10pm Sun Ⓜ Madou 🚼

Passage to India $$-$$$
Indian
Once you've come to terms with the frighteningly pink paint job, you're ready to enter the throng of expats and savour the vegetable thali, tandoori specialities or colonial-sounding *batata bara* (quail cooked with cream, coconut and raisins).
☎ 02 735 31 47 ✉ Chaussée de Louvain 223 🕑 noon-2.30pm & 6pm-midnight Ⓜ Madou ♿ fair 🚼 Ⓥ

Metin's the place for Turkish pizza

Entertainment

Au Bon Vieux Temps (p61)

Before going out in Brussels you need to choose which epoch you're in the mood to experience. Maybe you feel like stepping within the history-streaked walls of a century-old pub and drinking a beer brewed in an ancient monastery while surrounded by a cacophony of age-old tongues. Or perhaps you're in a grandiose frame of mind and prefer to sit among chandeliers and stained glass in a fabulous Art Nouveau café, waiting for a starched waiter to bring you a glass of eight-year-old gin and a Russian egg. Alternatively, sleek yourself up and strike a pose in a shiny, 'the-future-is-now' bar, club your way through a techno-filled night, catch some theatre in an Art Deco palace, some classical music in a circus, or an opera on the site of a revolution.

Entertainment venues are scattered across the Lower Town, with Place St Géry, Rue du Marché au Charbon and the streets immediately around Grand Place overflowing with bars, jazz and blues stages, and gregarious crowds. Not all the fun is indoors, however, as Brussels is also addicted to open-air events (see the boxed text on p60). One of the most enigmatic outdoor venues is Grand Place, which hosts concerts and unique spectacles such as the famous Tapis des Fleurs (Carpet of Flowers), when the cobblestones are covered in a blaze of begonias.

If you're not a fan of smoking, you'll struggle in the clouded air of many cafés and bars, though some (eg Le Cirio and Toone Estaminet) have a nonsmoking back room. It's worth noting that not everywhere accepts credit cards, and that many theatre and music venues hibernate over most of summer. A good place to check out what's on is, funnily enough, *What's On*, a supplement in the *Bulletin* (a weekly magazine, out on Thursday).

Solo Travellers

The unaccompanied will not attract any attention in Brussels for wandering around on their own. Besides the fact that Belgium is not one of those European nations where people are shocked to discover you don't have a spouse and at least five children with you at all times, this is also a city beleaguered by appointment-chasing businesspeople, so solo diners and drinkers are a common sight. The respect that Belgians have for individual privacy can be a double-edged sword – you're unlikely to be spontaneously earbashed by locals, but you may also find that a little effort is required to start up a conversation when you're in the mood to mingle.

Special Events

March *Ars Musica* – mid-March to early April; contemporary music festival occupying venues around Brussels, most notably Bozar (p67)

April *Serres Royales* – mid-April to early May; royal greenhouses reveal their spectacular flora to the public for a mere 10 days annually (see the boxed text on p28)
Festival du Film Bruxelles – late April to early May; 10-day festival of European cinema

May *Brussels Half-Marathon* – mid-May; more than 20,000 pairs of running shoes pound the capital's streets during this event
Brussels Jazz Marathon – last weekend in May; highly respected jazz convention held on stages all over the city
Kunsten Festival des Arts – mid-May to end May; Flemish and Wallonian music, dance, theatre and opera share the programme
Queen Elisabeth Competition – throughout May; prestigious classical event displaying young worldwide talent
Belgian Lesbian & Gay Pride – early May; also called Pink Saturday, a full-on glamour parade

June *Ommegang* – late June or early July; famous medieval procession from Place du Grand Sablon to a celebratory finish in Grand Place
Couleur Café Festival – last weekend in June; three-day festival of world music and dance

July *Foire de Midi* – mid-July to mid-August; fun-filled fair strung out along Boulevard du Midi, with stomach-churning rides and traditional food stalls
Palais Royal – mid-July to early September; once-a-year opportunity to see the royalty's palatial inner-city residence (p25)
Belgium National Day – 21 July; city-wide independence-day celebrations, with most of the fun centred around Parc de Bruxelles
Festival de Midis-Minimes – July to August; renowned festival of chamber, baroque and choral music (www.midis-minimes.be – French and Dutch only)

August *Meiboom* – 9 August; celebration of Brussels' defeat of Leuven in the 13th century, marked by a tree-planting at the corner of Rue des Sables and Rue du Marais
Tapis des Fleurs – mid-August; biennial three-day event when a brilliant floral carpet composed of 800,000 begonias is laid across Grand Place

September *Memorial Van Damme* – late August or early September; significant athletics meeting held in memory of Ivo Van Damme, a famous runner
Belgian Beer Weekend – early September; beer-tasting extravaganza in Grand Place

December *Marché de Noël* – first fortnight of December; grand Christmas market in Grand Place, with international craft stalls
Ice-skating – mid-December to end December; Grand Place is turned into an outdoor skating rink for two midwinter weeks

CAFÉS

Brussels is brimming with brown cafés (small, old-fashioned pubs), Art Nouveau cafés and *estaminets* (traditional cafés) – the best places to try an authentic brew.

À la Bécasse (2, D4) One of Brussels' atmospheric brown cafés, this is a one-room tavern that rapidly fills with tourists, locals, smoke and *lambic* stains. The tiled access alley is barely wide enough to admit a cat, much less swing one. A *bécasse* is a woodcock , which explains the bird-shaped motif on the footpath.
☎ **02 511 00 06** ✉ **Rue de Tabora 11, Lower Town** 🕑 **10am-midnight Mon-Sat, 11am-midnight Sun** Ⓜ **De Brouckère** 🚊 **Bourse premetro**

À la Mort Subite (2, F4) The name of this nicotine-tinted Art Nouveau café literally means 'instant death', but the only thing that dies in this sociable, beer-friendly hall is your ability to walk in a straight line, and even that dies slowly. There's also a beer called Mort Subite, but it's no more lethal than Belgium's other brews.
☎ **02 513 13 18** 💻 **www.alamortsubite.be** ✉ **Rue Montagne aux Herbes Potagères 7, Lower Town** 🕑 **11am-midnight** Ⓜ **Gare Centrale**

Au Bon Vieux Temps (2, D4) This is another quintessential brown café, with a secretive alleyway entrance to duck into, a cosy wood-panelled interior, two dozen beers to suck the froth off – including the tasty house brew, Vieux Temps – and a chain-smoking barkeep who seems as much a fixture as any of the café's 17th-century trimmings.
☎ **02 217 26 26** ✉ **Impasse Saint-Nicolas 4, off Rue du Marché aux Herbes 12** 🕑 **11am-midnight** Ⓜ **De Brouckère** 🚊 **Bourse premetro**

Falstaff (2, C4) This ravishing, century-old Art Nouveau café has fittings courtesy of well-known interior decorator Victor Horta. Ease yourself onto a well-padded banquette amid the pressed-metal ceilings, chandeliers and stained glass, and savour a Leffe Tripel in the style to which you are unaccustomed.
☎ **02 511 87 89** 💻 **www.resto.be/minisites/falstaff** ✉ **Rue Henri Maus 19, Lower Town** 🕑 **10am-2am** Ⓜ **De Brouckère** 🚊 **Bourse premetro**

Sip in style at Falstaff

La Fleur en Papier Doré (1, C4) This cigarette-packet-sized *estaminet* is brimming with old framed prints, photos and the graffiti of one-time regular Magritte and his surrealist pals. There's also plenty of beer and whisky with which to lubricate your gullet. Tourists are constantly dropping in, but regulars invariably form a tight knot around the bar.
☎ **02 511 16 59** ✉ **Rue des Alexiens 53, Lower Town** 🕑 **11am-8pm** Ⓜ **Gare Centrale** 🚊 **Anneessens premetro**

Le Cirio (2, C4) This authentic *belle époque* café is so gracious that no-one can bring themselves to drink to excess in here. Light meals include sardines, lasagne and Russian egg (hard-boiled egg with mayonnaise and salad), and the trademark drink is a *half-en-half*, a mixture of champagne and white wine.
☎ **02 512 13 95** ✉ **Rue de la Bourse 20, Lower Town** 🕑 **10am-1am** Ⓜ **De Brouckère** 🚊 **Bourse premetro** ♿ **fair**

Le Greenwich (2, B4) This old, mustard-walled, smoke-shrouded café is a sacred site for fanatical followers of that ultimate bourgeois blood sport – chess. Grandmaster Garry

Kasparov (no relation to Grandmaster Flash) once pondered his next move here, but nowadays it's mere mortals who hunch quietly over a chessboard and a cheap beer.
☎ 02 511 41 67 ✉ **Rue des Chartreux 7, Lower Town** 🕑 **10am-1am Sun-Thu, 10am-2am Fri & Sat** Ⓜ **Ste Catherine** 🚊 **Bourse premetro** ♿ **fair**

Toone Estaminet (2, E5) Beneath the Théâtre Royal de Toone (p32) is this great old *estaminet*, complete with enigmatic entrance, a nonsmoking back room, scattered bits of art and a clutch of outdoor tables. If you find yourself chatting to a marionette over a beer, it's time to leave.
☎ **02 511 71 37** 💻 **www.toone.be** ✉ **Impasse Schuddeveld 6 (Petite Rue des Bouchers 21), Lower Town** 🕑 **noon-midnight Feb-Dec** Ⓜ **De Brouckère** ☒

PUBS & BARS

Brasserie Ploegmans (1, C5) If you're interested in the social archaeology of the Marolles neighbourhood, visit this authentic working-class barroom, where tenured old drinkers creak their way to and from the bar through wisps of cheroot smoke, exchanging a few words of the impenetrable, fast-disappearing Bruxellois dialect along the way.
☎ **02 514 28 84** ✉ **Rue Haute 148, Marolles** 🕑 **2-10pm Mon-Sat** Ⓜ **Louise**

Goupil le Fol (2, D6) This wonderful, late-opening bar is best summed up by the French word *abracadabrant*: extraordinary and simultaneously incoherent. Dedicated to cabaret *chanteurs* (singers) like Piaf and Brel, the labyrinth of rooms is decorated with posters, old 45s and a blizzard of other paraphernalia. Much loved by locals, not least for its luscious fruit wines.
☎ **02 511 13 96** ✉ **Rue de la Violette 22, Lower Town** 🕑 **7.30pm-6am** Ⓜ **Gare Centrale**

Distilled Delight

Belgium's appreciation of alcoholic liquids doesn't stop at beer. *Jenever* (pronounced 'yenaiver'), a potent brew made from grain spirit, grasses and juniper berries, has been distilled here since the Middle Ages and is considered the precursor to modern-day gin. It was originally thought of as a health-giving drop due to the apparent medicinal powers of juniper, with drinkers gratefully accepting the placebo effect, but is now produced by more than 70 distilleries purely for leisure-time sipping. There are *jonge* (young) and *oude* (old) *jenevers*, with top-quality pale-yellow varieties maturing in barrels for at least eight years. Big-name producers include Filliers, St-Pol and Smeets.

All that jazz: L'Archiduc

L'Archiduc (2, B3) This is a classy, intimate Art Deco jazz lounge, with deep-blue booths to plunge into, finger-snapping background music and an upstairs balcony to chill out on. It serves up a soothing range of whiskeys, cognacs, bourbons and liqueurs, and has live music early Saturday evening. A great late-night haunt for aspiring insomniacs.
☎ **02 512 06 52** ✉ **Rue Antoine Dansaert 6, Lower Town** 🕑 **4pm-5am** Ⓜ **Ste Catherine** 🚊 **Bourse premetro**

Le Bier Circus (1, F3) Located next door to Cirque Royal (p67), this cluttered

Best Boozers

For a confused, utterly unreliable mixture of reasons involving atmosphere, the crowd, attitude of the staff, beer list, amount of alcohol drunk and sheer late-night *zeitgeist*, these are our top seven (five wasn't enough) places to drink in Brussels.

- L'Archiduc (opposite)
- Goupil le Fol (opposite)
- Au Bon Vieux Temps (p61)
- Moeder Lambic (below)
- La Fleur en Papier Doré (p61)
- Zebra (below)
- Le Cirio (p61)

old pub dispenses drinking advice and more than 200 beers (from Abbaye des Rocs to Zatte Bie) to expert quaffers and novices alike. It extends the brewery theme to the bar's menu, from which you can order beer-cooked *moules* (mussels).
☎ **02 218 00 34** 💻 **www.biercircus.com (French only)** ✉ **Rue de l'Enseignement 89, Upper Town** 🕐 **noon-2.30pm & 6pm-midnight Mon-Fri** Ⓜ **Madou**

Mappa Mundo (2, B4) This is part of the triad of trendy Frédéric Nicolay–created drinking spots (Zebra and Roi des Belges are the other two) that have brought barflies swarming to Place St Géry. Forget the concept (cynical world traveller falls for smoky-voiced cabaret singer) and just settle into a comfy, cushioned cubicle with a fistful of Duvel.
☎ **02 514 35 55** ✉ **Rue du Pont de la Carpe 2, Lower Town** 🕐 **1pm-late** Ⓜ **De Brouckère** 🚋 **Bourse premetro**

Moeder Lambic (Map p33) On your way to or from Musée Horta (p16), drop in to this unpretentious tavern to leaf through the black folder detailing its startling line-up of hundreds of Belgian beers. Alternatively, leaf through the old comic books jammed behind the front windows or just stare admiringly at the empty bottles lining the walls.
☎ **02 539 14 19** ✉ **Rue de Savoie 68, St Gilles** 🕐 **4pm-late Mon-Sat** Ⓜ **Porte de Hal** 🚋 **Horta premetro** ♿ **fair**

O'Reilly's (2, C4) Sports-hungry foreigners shoulder their way into the cool, dark-wooded interior of this formulaic but friendly Irish pub to digest hours of loudly televised rugby and football coverage. No prizes for guessing what's on the beer menu.
☎ **02 552 04 80** ✉ **Place de la Bourse 1, Lower Town** 🕐 **11am-late** Ⓜ **De Brouckère** 🚋 **Bourse premetro**

Roi des Belges (2, B4) Another of the bars on Place St Géry striving to be the coolest thing since yesterday's coolest thing, this place is half old-time bar and half slick bistro. Friendly bar staff make a relaxed counterpoint to the self-conscious preeners and casually fashionable bystanders loitering over its two floors.
☎ **02 503 43 00** ✉ **Rue Jules Van Praet 35, Lower Town** 🕐 **11am-late** Ⓜ **De Brouckère** 🚋 **Bourse premetro**

Zebra (2, B4) Rough-around-the-edges brickwork and beaten-metal tables give Zebra a fashionably gritty feel, while the food is good and cheap. On Thursday night there's live 'bossa', jazz and funk (entry free); at other times you may hear what sounds like a bunch of drunken synthesizers getting acquainted.
☎ **02 511 09 01** ✉ **Place St Géry 35, Lower Town** 🕐 **noon-2am** Ⓜ **De Brouckère** 🚋 **Bourse premetro** ♿ **fair**

DANCE CLUBS

Bazaar (1, C6) Once you've eaten your fill in the extravagant upstairs restaurant (p53), head downstairs into the cavernous basement club to catch some rock, funk, soul and a little disco fever. The music won't necessarily set your feet or your imagination on fire, but you'll bump into plenty of other foreigners.
☎ 02 511 26 00 ✉ **Rue des Capucins 63, Marolles** € **€8** 🕑 **7.30pm-late Thu-Sat** M **Porte de Hal**

Fuse (1, B6) This rambling club is Brussels' biggest house and techno affair (one floor is devoted to each), where a polished line-up of international and Belgian DJs with hallucinogenic names (Spacid, Psychogene, Mellow) flagellate the eardrums of their young audience. It's open on Saturday, when a big crowd makes the most of it.
☎ 02 511 97 89 💻 **www.fuse.be** ✉ **Rue Blaes 208, Marolles** € **11pm-midnight €2.50, midnight-7am €8** 🕑 **11pm-7am Sat** M **Porte de Hal**

L'Espace de Nuit (2, E6) This tourist-favoured disco covers several floors and prefers retro music that's already proven itself on the pop charts. Its neon display is located only a block from Grand Place, sandwiched between the fast-food emporiums on 'pitta street'.
☎ **02 502 76 89** ✉ **Rue du Marché aux Fromages 10, Lower Town** € **€6** 🕑 **10pm-late** M **Gare Centrale**

Mirano (1, F3) This place is big, bold and brash – a self-image shared by the resident clubbers. It recently renewed its dance club credentials (after some time out) with the popular 'Dirty Dancing', which sees a blend of house, electro and *disco nouveau* pumped out by some talented DJs.
☎ **02 227 39 41** 💻 **www.mirano.be** ✉ **Chaussée de Louvain 38, St Josse** € **10.30pm-midnight €5, midnight-4am €10** 🕑 **10.30pm-4am Sat** M **Madou**

Take your pick of house or techno at Fuse

CINEMAS

Cinéma Arenberg-Galeries (2, E5) This cinema of the arts has an eclectic programme of new releases and re-releases, and an excellent summer festival of classics and previously unscreened contemporary works called Ecran Total. There were doubts about the theatre's future at the time of research, but hopefully this great venue will persevere.
☎ **02 512 80 63** 💻 **www.arenberg.be (French & Dutch only)** ✉ **Galerie de la Reine 26, Lower Town** € **adult/concession €6.60/5.20** M **Gare Centrale** ♿ **fair** 👶

Drive-In Cinema (3, D2) Every summer, the turf beside the Arcade du Cinquantenaire is transformed into a weekend drive-in screening recent hits, with food and drinks distributed before the movie. If you turn up on foot, your rebelliousness will be rewarded with a chair and a set of headphones.
💻 **www.basedrivein.be (French & Dutch only)** ✉ **L'Esplanade du Cinquantenaire, EU Area** € **car/pedestrian €15/2** 🕑 **from 8pm Fri & Sat Jul-Aug** M **Mérode** ♿ **good** 👶

Kinepolis (Map p35) Hugely popular at weekends, Kinepolis is a garishly lit multiplex in the Bruparck

Kinepolis multiplex

complex. It has two dozen screens on which the latest US releases compete, plus a seven-storey IMAX experience.
☎ 02 474 26 00 🖳 www.kinepolis.be ✉ **Bruparck, Blvd du Centenaire 20, Laeken € adult/child/student €7.20/5.70/5.70 M Heysel ♿ good 🚼**

UGC Cinéma (2, D1) This cinema has 12 *salles* (halls) of movie-going entertainment, usually mainstream American schlockbusters, though low-budget flicks and European art-house reels sometimes sneak in through the back door and screen themselves when no-one's watching.
☎ 0900 104 40 🖳 **www.ugc.be (French & Dutch only) ✉ Place de Brouckère 38, Lower Town € adult/student/child €7.20/5.60/5.60 M De Brouckère ♿ good 🚼**

ROCK, JAZZ & BLUES

Ancienne Belgique (2, B5) The venerable 'AB' hosts several auditoriums' worth of local and world music. Recent programmes confirm that most tastes are catered for, with performers as varied as Motorhead, the Eels, Goldfrapp and French pretty boy Benjamin Biolay all making appearances here.
☎ 02 548 24 24 🖳 **www.abconcerts.be ✉ Blvd Anspach 110, Lower Town; box office: Rue des Pierres 23 € €10-25 ⏲ box office 11am-4pm Mon-Fri M De Brouckère 🚊 Bourse premetro ♿ fair**

Bizon (2, B4) There must be a reason why there's a bison head on the back wall and a motorbike on the ceiling, but it's not immediately apparent. What is clear is that this bar loves its blues. Monday night usually sees a professional jam session, while Tuesday night has live music after 7pm.
☎ 02 502 46 99 🖳 **www.cafebizon.com ✉ Rue du Pont de la Carpe 7, Lower Town € free ⏲ 6pm-late M De Brouckère 🚊 Bourse premetro**

Magasin 4 (1, C1) This place was established 10 years ago on the corner of Rue du Magasin and Rue des Commerçants to counter the city's appetite for 1980s hits and mod-pop mulch. It plays so-called alternative sounds: punk, neo-metal, hardcore, industrial, ska, experimental, drum 'n' bass or fusions of these and other styles.
☎ 02 223 34 74 🖳 **www.artagenda.be/magasin4 (French only) ✉ Rue du Magasin 4, Lower Town € €5-15 ⏲ concerts usually from 8pm Thu-Sat M Yser**

Music Village (2, C5) Belgian blues singer Marc Lelangue, sax-men Bart Defoort and Toon Roos, Nathalie Loriers' jazz sextet and jazz vocalist Florence Antraygues are just some of the musical talent that has

Ne Me Quitte Pas

Belgium's musical claims to fame include Adolphe Sax, who in 1842 invented a distinctive reed instrument. But nobody is better known here than raspy-voiced Jacques Brel. Born in 1929, Brel cut his teeth at 23 in the Brussels cabaret La Rose Noire. He was soon in Paris mingling with the likes of Edith Piaf and by 1955 his stardom was confirmed. The French tried to claim Brel as their own, a feeling not completely unrequited (Brel named his daughter France), but he often acknowledged his homeland in the verses of his passion-wracked songs. Brel died of cancer in 1978; his spirit lives on at the Fondation Jaques Brel (p21).

recently graced the stage of this youthful club. Young European performers are regularly given the spotlight.
☎ 02 513 13 45 💻 www.themusicvillage.com
✉ Rue des Pierres 50, Lower Town € €6-20
🕑 performances usually from 8pm Wed-Sat
Ⓜ De Brouckère
🚊 Bourse premetro

Sounds (1, F6) Lounging in the suburban wilds of Ixelles is this informal jazz venue, visited by local performers and out-of-towners desperate to break into the small-time. Contemporary jazz is the usual sound of choice.
☎ 02 512 92 50 💻 www.jazzvalley.com/sounds
✉ Rue de la Tulipe 28, Ixelles € up to €12
🕑 noon-late Mon-Fri, 7pm-late Sat Oct-Jun; performances from 10pm daily Oct-Jun
Ⓜ Porte de Namur

VK (1, B1) VK (De Vaartkapoen) thrives on reggae, hip-hop, rap, world music and indie rock bands. It's not the most salubrious part of town to be in after a late-finishing concert – be prepared to nab yourself a cab.
☎ 02 414 29 07 💻 www.vaartkapoen.be (Dutch only) ✉ Rue de l'Ecole 76, Molenbeek-St-Jean
€ €7-20
Ⓜ Comte de Flandre

THEATRE & DANCE

Beursschouwburg (2, B4) The Beursschouwburg has recently been confined to its quarters while renovations are performed on every visible surface. It's expected to resume its presentation of contemporary music – from rap to left-of-centre rock to jazz and back again – in the first half of 2004.
☎ 02 513 82 90 💻 www.beursschouwburg.be (French & Dutch only)
✉ Rue Auguste Orts 20-28, Lower Town
€ from €7 🕑 box office 10am-6pm Mon-Fri Ⓜ De Brouckère 🚊 Bourse premetro ♿ good

Halles de Schaerbeek (1, F1) This massive 1901 hall, formerly the site of the Marché Ste Marie food market, is now a performing-arts venue featuring rock concerts, contemporary installations, innovative modern choreography and film screenings.
☎ 02 218 21 07 💻 www.halles.be (French only)

Beursschouwburg

✉ Rue Royale Ste Marie 22, Schaerbeek; box office: Rue de la Constitution 20
€ €10-25 🕑 box office 2-6pm Mon-Fri
Ⓜ Botanique ♿ fair

Théâtre National/ Le Palace (1, D2/2, B4) The immense new National Theatre being built on Boulevard Emile Jacqmain is expected to be inaugurated in September 2004. Until then, the theatre of the city's French population is housed in an Art Deco cinema called Le Palace, where it often shows previously unstaged Wallonian works.
☎ 02 203 53 03, box office 02 203 41 55 💻 www.theatrenational.be (French only) ✉ Théâtre National: Blvd Emile Jacqmain, Lower Town; Le Palace: Blvd Anspach 85, Lower Town; box office: 2nd fl, Rue des Poissonniers 11-13, Lower Town € adult/child from €15/7.50 🕑 box office 11am-6pm Tue-Sat mid-Aug to mid-Jul Ⓜ De Brouckère 🚊 Bourse premetro ♿ good 🚸

Théâtre Royal du Parc (1, E4) Nestled in the northeastern corner of Parc de Bruxelles is this attractive thespian hang-out, a favourite of the city's theatre-goers. Recent seasons have been dominated by adaptations of the comedic works of the likes of Moliere and Eugene O'Neill. Matinees start at 3pm, while evening shows begin at 8pm.
☎ info 02 505 30 40, box office 02 505 30 30
💻 www.theatreduparc.be
✉ Rue de la Loi 3, Upper Town € €5-29 🕑 box office 11am-6pm Sep-May
Ⓜ Parc ♿ fair

CLASSICAL MUSIC & OPERA

Cirque Royal (1, F3) After tiring of its life as an indoor circus, this venue ran away from itself to become a unique performance space for classical and modern music, opera and dance. Recent high-profile events have included an Elvis Costello gig and St Petersburg's Rimsky-Korsakov ballet troupe performing *Swan Lake*.
☎ 02 218 20 15 ✉ Rue de l'Enseignement 81, Upper Town € €10-85 ⏲ box office 10.30am-6pm Mon-Sat, also opens 1hr before performances M Madou ♿ good

Conservatoire Royal de Bruxelles (1, D5) The city's respected music conservatory has its own grand concert hall and is a prime venue for classical music. Conservatory programmes can also include jazz gigs and piano recitals, and the institution participates in a mightily popular musical celebration called the Festival de Midis-Minimes (p60).
☎ 02 511 04 27 💻 www.conservatoire.be (French only) ✉ Rue de la Régence 30, Sablon € adult/student from €10/6 ⏲ concerts usually begin 8pm M Louise ♿ fair

Le Botanique (1, F2) Inaugurated in 1984, the Centre Culturel de la Communauté Française (French Community Cultural Centre) keeps its grand former greenhouse and various other halls and galleries busy with a highly refined international programme of concerts (classical, rock and pop), theatre, dance and cinema.
☎ 02 218 37 32, 02 226 12 11 💻 www.botanique.be (French & Dutch only) ✉ Rue Royale 236, St Josse € €10-35 ⏲ from 9am Mon-Fri, from 10am Sat & Sun; closes 7pm or when events finish M Botanique ♿ fair

Palais des Beaux-Arts (Bozar) (1, E4) The Centre for Fine Arts is a distinguished, Horta-designed, Art Deco venue, an inspirational setting for a programme of classical music, dance, theatre and art exhibitions. The 2200-seat Salle Henry Le Bœuf is regularly serenaded by Belgium's National Orchestra. In a clumsy attempt at modernisation, the centre recently adopted the clownish contraction 'Bozar'.
☎ info 02 507 84 44, box office 02 507 82 00 💻 www.bozar.be (French & Dutch only) ✉ Rue Ravenstein 23, Upper Town; box office: Rue Ravenstein 5 € varies according to performance ⏲ box office 11am-7pm Mon-Sat, until 8.30pm performance nights M Parc ♿ good

Théâtre Royal de la Monnaie (2, E3) La Monnaie (De Munt to the Flemish) is Belgium's premier opera venue. The fetching neoclassical facade is the only surviving remnant of the original 1817 building, razed by a fire in 1855. Good tickets are expensive, but remember that the acoustics were good enough to launch a revolution in 1830 (see the boxed text at left).
☎ 02 229 12 00, box office 070 23 39 39 💻 www.lamonnaie.be ✉ Place de la Monnaie, Lower Town € performances €7.50-150; opera house tours adult/child/student €6/3/4 ⏲ box office 11am-6pm Tue-Sat; tours noon Sat Sep-Dec & Mar-Jun M De Brouckère ♿ good

A Revolutionary Performance

On 25 August 1830, La Monnaie hosted the premiere of *La Muette de Portici* (The Dumb Girl of Portici), by Daniel-François-Esprit Auber, a dramatic spectacle telling the story of Naples' 1647 uprising against the Spanish. It proved too much for a city tired of Dutch rule. During a patriotic song trumpeting a 'sacred love of the homeland', the audience stampeded into the streets and, helped by other discontents, hoisted the Brabant flag over the Hôtel de Ville. A month later the Dutch conceded defeat, and Belgian independence was officially recognised in January 1831.

GAY & LESBIAN BRUSSELS

Chez Maman (2, B6) The drag shows at this snug cabaret bar are an entertaining indulgence for queers and nonqueers alike, with the show queens high-heeling it energetically through (and on) the furnishings. Get there early to catch the camp.
☎ 02 502 86 96 ✉ Rue des Grands Carmes 7, Lower Town € from €8 ⏲ 10pm-late Thu-Sun M De Brouckère 🚊 Bourse premetro

La Démence (1, B6) 'The Madness' takes hold one day each month, when the Fuse club relinquishes its interior to a chaotic gay rave with a formidable reputation among locals, as well as among international party-goers who bus in from places like Amsterdam and Paris.
☎ 02 511 97 89 💻 www.lademence.com ✉ Fuse, Rue Blaes 208, Marolles € 10-11pm €8, 11pm-noon €13 ⏲ 10pm-noon one day per month M Porte de Hal

Social anthropology: L'Homo Erectus

Le Belgica (2, C5) This pub has an old-fashioned look but a new-fashioned bunch of attendees. It's a good place to overhear information on gay events, listen to DJs and savour Belgian beer.
💻 www.lebelgica.be ✉ Rue du Marché au Charbon 32, Lower Town ⏲ 10pm-3am Thu-Sun M De Brouckère 🚊 Bourse premetro

L'Homo Erectus (2, C5) The goal of this heavily patronised bar is social evolution, and customers pursue this aim with vigour while crowded around the modest interior. It's often packed at week's end, and its website has lots of gay information.
☎ 02 514 74 93 💻 www.lhomoerectus.com (French only) ✉ Rue des Pierres 57, Lower Town ⏲ noon-6am Mon-Fri, 2pm-6am Sat & Sun M De Brouckère 🚊 Bourse premetro

Underground Kafé (2, C5) The name could be a hint that this place is willing to get down and dirty. The cosy inner sanctum is home to drag shows every Friday and Saturday night, and a noisy, uninhibited ambience.
☎ 02 503 11 60 💻 www.undergroundkafe.com (French only) ✉ Rue des Pierres 45, Lower Town ⏲ 4pm-3am Mon-Thu, 4pm-5am Fri & Sat, 4pm-1am Sun M De Brouckère 🚊 Bourse premetro

SPORTS

Roi Baudouin Stadium (Map p35) Brussels' main stadium was originally called Heysel, but was renamed after the 1985 European Cup final when a riot involving Liverpool and Juventus football fans led to the deaths of 35 people. Besides international football matches and other sports events like the athletic meeting Memorial Van Damme, the 50,000-seat stadium also hosts big-name concerts.
☎ 02 474 39 40 💻 www.fsb.be ✉ Ave du Marathon, Heysel € €10-85 M Roi Baudouin ♿ fair

Vandenstock Stadium The distinctive purple tunics you occasionally see around Brussels belong to supporters of RSC Anderlecht, the city's most famous football team. Seeing them play at their Vandenstock home ground is an experience sports-lovers shouldn't miss.
☎ 02 522 15 39 💻 www.anderlecht-online.be ✉ Ave Théo Verbeeck 2, Anderlecht € football tickets €15-30 ⏲ box office 9am-6pm Mon-Fri, 10am-noon Sat M St Guidon ♿ fair 🚸

Sleeping

Although Europe's summer months from May to September see accommodation getting heavily booked in most parts of Belgium, in Brussels the reverse is true: the city's population of Eurocrats and associated businesspeople go missing in action over the holiday break, as well as on weekends year round, leaving many hotel rooms to be filled. See the boxed text on p73 for more information.

Hotels in Brussels are expensive by general European standards, but this means that the rooms (*chambre* in French, *kamer* in Flemish) on offer in even budget hotels are usually clean, well maintained and reasonably comfortable. At the other end of the accommodation spectrum, the deluxe and top-end hotels that have bred like rabbits since the EU moved into town with its luxury-seeking entourage have the full range of amenities, which can include 24-hour room service, fitness and business centres, Internet data points, baby-sitting, pet approval (also common in mid-range places) and nonsmoking floors. Mid-range places are generally older, with mix-and-match facilities, but what they lack in predictability they often make up for with fuss-free service and appealingly eccentric personas – examples include the Hotel Noga, Hotel Mozart and Comfort Art Hotel Siru (all p72).

Room Rates

The prices in this chapter indicate the cost per night of a standard double room in high season.

Deluxe	over €350
Top End	€150 to €350
Mid-Range	€85 to €149
Budget	under €85

Most mid-range places and a surprising number of top-end digs forgo an on-site eatery, excepting the breakfast room (breakfast is usually included in the room price). This isn't a problem, however, because of the spread and diversity of restaurants and cafés across the city centre. Facilities for people in wheelchairs are sorely lacking in Brussels' hotels, even in some of the top-notch establishments – barrier-free rooms do exist (eg the Marriott; p71), but often the best that hotels can offer are *chambres* with a doorway allowing wheelchair access.

Accommodation in Brussels attracts a 6% value-added tax (VAT), which is incorporated into your bill. For information on booking services, see the boxed text on p71.

The opulent entrance hall of the Hôtel Métropole (p70)

DELUXE

Conrad (1, D6) Can't bring yourself to take a shower unless the bathroom is made of marble? Or sleep unless the pillow is oversized, relax unless there's a *hamman* (bath house) and a pool nearby, or check in unless the lobby has a chandelier? Then this is the place for you.
02 542 48 00 www.conradhotels.com Ave Louise 71, Ixelles Louise good Café Wiltcher

Hotel Amigo (2, D6) It's hard to get more central than this newly refurbished high-class hotel, part of the Rocco Forte chain and situated across the road from the Hôtel de Ville's backside. The rooms have an appealing modern design and the well-equipped fitness centre will ensure you stay in shape while you relax.
02 547 47 47 www.hotelamigo.com Rue de l'Amigo 1-3, Lower Town Gare Centrale Bourse premetro fair Bocconi Ristorante Italiano

Hotel Astoria (1, E3) The weighty, early-20th-century grandeur descends on you the moment you march into the magnificent foyer, and then pursues you past Art Deco skylights, fabulous furnishings and a Louis XIV-style restaurant all the way to your spacious, mod-con-filled suite.

Live in luxury: the Conrad

02 227 05 05 www.sofitel.com Rue Royale 103, Upper Town Botanique fair Le Palais Royal

Hôtel Métropole (2, E2) The late-19th-century exterior of this superswish, 'fetch me my Lear jet' establishment is unremarkable, but inside it's a different story, most notably the marble, teak and crystal opulence of the French Renaissance-style entrance and reception halls. Fortunately for your overloaded senses, the modern bedrooms are more restrained in style.
02 217 23 00 www.metropolehotel.be Place de Brouckère 31, Lower Town De Brouckère good Café Métropole (p49)

Royal Windsor Hotel (2, E6) Mahogany and oak abound in this fastidious old-school hotel, located within two blocks of Grand Place. High-speed Internet connection is a standard feature of the bedchambers and there's also a well-equipped business centre. If you're in a regal mood, snap up the Royal Suite for €1400 per night.
02 505 55 55 www.royalwindsorbrussels.com Rue Duquesnoy 5, Lower Town Gare Centrale Chutney's

Stanhope (1, F5) This is Belgium's original five-star hotel, a threesome of late-19th-century townhouses decorated in the best tradition of English to-the-manor-born style, with leather club chairs, meandering ivy in the garden and classically furnished rooms with an excess of floral fabrics. To stay here, you must wear jodhpurs and be accompanied by a foxhound.
02 506 91 11 www.benotel.com/belgium/brussels/stanhope Rue du Commerce 9, Upper Town Trône fair Brighton Restaurant

Le Dixseptième

TOP END

Bedford (1, C4) This hotel has more than 300 comfortable, nonexotic rooms for those who can't stand another night in a grand period bedroom. It has a compact exercise centre, a high-standard French restaurant and a piano bar where you can attempt a martini-fuelled re-enactment of *The Fabulous Baker Boys*.
☎ 02 507 00 00 🖳 www.hotelbedford.be ✉ Rue du Midi 135-137, Lower Town Ⓜ Gare du Midi 🚊 Anneessens premetro ✕ Magellan 👶

Hôtel Manos Stéphanie (Map p33) This hotel advertises itself as being right in the centre of the city, but its location a block from Avenue Louise is a respectable walk from Grand Place. It has elegant Louis XV- and XVI-style room decorations, antique-stuffed corridors, very professional staff and an unhurried air.
☎ 02 539 02 50 🖳 www.manoshotel.com/stephanie ✉ Chaussée de Charleroi 28, St Gilles Ⓜ Louise ✕ Les Jardins des Bagatelle (p52) 👶

Le Dixseptième (2, E6) These beautifully restored 15th-century lodgings have a tranquil air that belies their closeness to Grand Place, as well as thoroughly modern facilities including free Internet access in every room and plasma-screen TVs in most. The majority of guests make return bookings, so reserve a room well in advance of your visit.
☎ 02 517 17 17 🖳 www.ledixseptieme.be ✉ Rue de la Madeleine 25, Lower Town Ⓜ Gare Centrale ✕ Sea Grill (p50) 👶

Marriott (2, C4) This is a comfortably predictable, business-friendly member of a top-end hotel chain, though the supposed prestige of staying here is diluted by the prominence of a fast-food franchise in the same building. It has one barrier-free room, plus a wheelchair-accessible room on each floor. Significantly discounted walk-in rates are often available.
☎ 02 516 90 90 🖳 www.marriott.com ✉ Rue Auguste Orts 3-7, Lower Town Ⓜ De Brouckère 🚊 Bourse premetro ♿ good ✕ Brasserie Le Sauvoir 👶

Meliá Avenue Louise (Map p33) This small, sumptuous boutique hotel has around 80 restful rooms and suites on offer, utilised mainly by those who are in Brussels to do business with the various major companies headquartered nearby. Staying here makes you feel important, even if you're not. The generous breakfast buffet costs an extra €22.
☎ 02 535 95 00 🖳 www.solmelia.com ✉ Rue Blanche 4, Ixelles Ⓜ Louise ✕ L'Amadeus 👶

Novotel Brussels Centre – Tour Noire (2, C2) Wrapped around a tower that was part of Brussels' original fortifications, this hotel is visually impressive. It's also statistically impressive, with more than 200 rooms (including three barrier-free rooms), containing what the brochure calls 'the new concept of bathroom'. There's another Novotel near Grand Place, on Place d'Espagne.
☎ 02 505 50 50 🖳 www.novotel.com ✉ Rue de la Vierge Noire 32, Lower Town Ⓜ De Brouckère ♿ excellent ✕ Côté Jardin 👶

Accommodation Agencies

The **TIB** (2, D5; ☎ 02 513 89 40; 🕑 9am-6pm) has a accommodation counter in its office on Grand Place; the service is free (you pay a deposit but it's deducted from your room rate). **Bed & Brussels** (Map p33; ☎ 02 646 07 37; www.bnb-brussels.be; Rue Kindermans 9, Ixelles) is a friendly, professional service connecting the city's growing B&B accommodation with overnighting visitors. About 10% of its listings are in the centre, with the rest equally distributed in Brussels' south, north and east. Double rooms cost from €55 to €95 per night and €320 to €550 per week.

Renaissance Brussels Hotel (1, F5) The exterior is hardly an architectural renaissance, but inside are plush modern rooms, a business centre and a pool-equipped fitness realm. The hotel gets a lot of its business from executive types with appointments around the corner in the EU area. It can also book you into the executive apartment complex next door.
☎ 02 505 29 29 🖳 **www.renaissancehotels.com** ✉ **Rue du Parnasse 19, Upper Town** Ⓜ **Trône** ♿ **good** ✕ **Symphony** 🚼

MID-RANGE

Atlas (2, A3) Its efficient staff and quiet location near the placid Place Ste Catherine, around the corner from the boutiques of Rue Antoine Dansaert, make Atlas a handy choice. The décor is nothing flash, excepting the bits of 14th-century city wall incorporated into the breakfast room.
☎ 02 502 60 06 🖳 **www.atlas-hotel.be** ✉ **Rue du Vieux Marché aux Grains 30, Lower Town** Ⓜ **Ste Catherine** ♿ **fair** ✕ **Le Paon Royal (p56)** 🚼

Comfort Art Hotel Siru (1, D1) This weathered, Art Deco–fronted hotel, which clashes with the ho-hum modernity of the surrounding business area, used the imaginations of 130 contemporary artists to decorate its rooms. The result is sometimes cheesy, but mostly refreshingly different from the production-line aesthetics of other hotels.
☎ 02 203 35 80 🖳 **www.comforthotelsiru.com** ✉ **Place Rogier 1, St Josse** Ⓜ **Rogier** ✕ **Brasserie St Germain**

Hotel le Dôme (1, D2) This green-tinged, Art Nouveau hotel offers comfortable, well-equipped bedrooms. Those who live to shop will appreciate the quick access to the retail outlets on Rue Neuve. It's also called Le Dôme 1 due to the existence of a sibling hotel (Le Dôme II) a few doors down.
☎ 02 218 06 80 🖳 **www.hotel-le-dome.be** ✉ **Blvd du Jardin Botanique 12-13, Lower Town** Ⓜ **Rogier** ✕ **Cafe du Dôme** 🚼

Hotel Mozart (2, E6) The rooms are charming and well maintained, but the real reason you should stay here is to prowl the salmon-mousse-coloured corridors creaking with antique furnishings and paintings, while enjoying a soundtrack of piped concertos. Legend has it that Wolfgang Amadeus Mozart has absolutely no connection to this hotel.
☎ 02 502 66 61 🖳 **www.hotel-mozart.be** ✉ **Rue du Marché aux Fromages 23, Lower Town** Ⓜ **Gare Centrale** ✕ **Al Barmaki (p49)** 🚼

Hotel Noga (2, B1) This delightful hotel was furnished by someone with an eccentric yet playful eye, hence the cosy jumble of old books, paintings, cabinets, gramophones and other eclectic bits and pieces. It also has a snooker parlour, friendly staff and modern spacious rooms to rest up in.
☎ 02 218 67 63 🖳 **www.nogahotel.com** ✉ **Rue du Béguinage 38, Lower Town** Ⓜ **Ste Catherine** ✕ **Le Vistro (p56)** 🚼

Hôtel Saint Michel (2, E6) Grand Place's sole hotel is tucked away in the splendid Le Maison des Ducs de Brabant. Ignore the narrow, scuffed corridors and instead acknowledge the helpful staff and 15 comfortable rooms, half of which yield rare views over Brussels' main attraction.

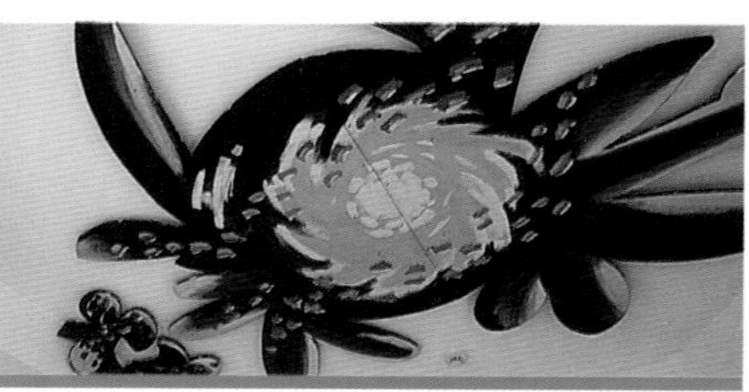
Artistic touches at the Comfort Art Hotel Siru

Rooms facing Grand Place cost €30 to €40 more.
☎ 02 511 09 56 🖳 **www.accueilettraditiongrandplace.be** ✉ **Grand Place 15, Lower Town** Ⓜ **De Brouckère** 🚊 **Bourse premetro** ✖ **La Maison du Cygne (p49)** 🚼

La Légende (2, C6) This particular legend dates back only to 1957, though it inhabits an 18th-century building. The hotel is a warm, family-run affair with modern rooms within sniffing distance of Grand Place. The city centre can be a festive place, so try for a room facing into the quiet inner courtyard.
☎ 02 512 82 90 🖳 **www.hotellalegende.com** ✉ **Rue du Lombard 35, Lower Town** Ⓜ **Gare Centrale** 🚊 **Bourse premetro** ✖ **Le Bar à Tapas (p57)**

BUDGET

Chambres en Ville (1, F5) Hidden in a quiet corner of the Upper Town is this very popular B&B – book well in advance. It has four cosy rooms, each decorated according to a sweeping theme such as 'life of an artist' or 'back from Africa'. Single-night stays attract a €12 surcharge.
☎ 02 512 92 90 ✉ **Rue de Londres 19, Upper Town** Ⓜ **Trône** ✖ **L'Estran (p52)**

Hôtel À La Grande Cloche (1, C4) This commendable hotel on quiet Place Rouppe is centrally located yet outside the hubbub of the city centre. It has a pleasant muted colour scheme and the rooms are decently sized for the price bracket. Rooms with bathroom can cost up to €25 extra per night.
☎ 02 512 61 40 🖳 **www.hotelgrandecloche.com** ✉ **Place Rouppe 10, Marolles** Ⓜ **Gare du Midi** 🚊 **Anneessens premetro** ✖ **La Grande Porte (p54)**

Hotel Galia (1, C5) This hotel is hoping to expand its quota of rooms from 25 to 40, good news for those who like personable, well-maintained accommodation. There are *bande dessinée* (comic strip) embellishments throughout the hotel, which overlooks an impressive morning flea market.
☎ 02 502 42 43 🖳 **www.hotelgalia.com (French only)** ✉ **Place du Jeu de Balle 15-16, Marolles** Ⓜ **Porte de Hal** ✖ **Brasserie la Clef d'Or (p53)**

Hôtel Rembrandt (1, E6) Though not picture perfect, this budget hotel does have a certain history-charged charm due to the old-style furnishings and artworks that adorn its rooms. The more expensive rooms come with private toilet and bathtub.
☎ 02 512 71 39 ✉ **Rue de la Concorde 42, Ixelles** Ⓜ **Louise** ✖ **Havana Corner (p51)** 🚼

Sleep Well (1, E2) This large, bright and busy hostel has an uninspiring but central location close to Place des Martyrs. Standard one- to four-person rooms come with sheets and breakfast, and you're locked out from 11am to 3pm. The newer, more expensive Pullman rooms have their own facilities and no lock-out.
☎ 02 218 50 50 🖳 **www.sleepwell.be** ✉ **Rue du Damier 23, Lower Town** Ⓜ **Rogier** ♿ **good** ✖ **L'Intermezzo (p50)**

Cheap Sleeps

The prices in many of Brussels' corporate-inclined hotels can be dramatically reduced over the weekend (often by 30% to 50%), when their core clientele of visiting EU personnel and businesspeople stay at home. Another great period for low prices is the summer holidays (roughly the last week of July through August), when many businesses close temporarily and the hotel trade dries up. During these times, some hotels continue to quote their 'rack rates' (official advertised rates) over the phone and on websites, but it's a different story if you walk in off the street.

About Brussels

HISTORY

Present-day Brussels was first settled by real-estate-savvy Neolithic types from around 2250 BC. The Romans also lived here for 500 years, but were booted out by Germanic Franks. In 695, bishop St Géry erected a chapel on an island in the swampy River Senne (Zenne), which grew into a settlement called Bruocsella: from *bruoc* (swamp) and *sella* (dwelling). In the mid-9th century, Charlemagne's empire was divided into bits corresponding roughly to Germany, France and the Low Countries, setting the scene for the divide that would eventually become modern-day French-speaking Wallonia and Flemish-speaking Flanders.

The feudal counts of Flanders began exerting influence in the late 9th century, building fortresses in Ghent and Bruges. While Flanders was rising, infant Brussels received the Coudenberg Palace in the 11th century, followed by the construction of a 4km-long defensive wall. Brussels outgrew its urban playpen by the 14th century, when a second pentagon-shaped wall was built, twice as long as the first. By this time, local feudalism was declining while towns like Bruges and Ypres were bursting with cloth-trade wealth and rich merchants.

The 14th-century Porte de Hal (p25)

The 15th-century reign of French king Philip the Good was conducted partly from Brussels, which he embellished with a Grand Place and a new sense of culture. But the 16th century saw a Protestant rethink of Catholic edicts (the Reformation) and subsequent Low Country revolts against the Spanish Catholic rule. Nonetheless, Brussels became capital of the Spanish Netherlands in 1585. More pan-European bloodshed followed, including the bombardment of Brussels by Marshal De Villeroy in 1695, which virtually wiped out Grand Place (see the boxed text on p9).

The ruling Austrian Habsburgs spent the 18th century fostering much urban development in Brussels, including Place Royale and most of the Upper Town's other architectural highlights. The French took over in 1794 and incorporated the area into France, but Napoleon Bonaparte's defeat at Waterloo in 1815 led to the creation of the United Kingdom of the Netherlands, incorporating Holland, Belgium and Luxembourg. A mere 15 years later, after attempts by King William I to make Dutch the national language, inciting both French and Flemish speakers, the Belgians revolted and sent the Dutch packing (see the boxed text on p67).

Belgian independence was recognised by the rest of Europe in January 1831 at the Conference of London, and on 21 July King Léopold I was inaugurated. The nation's first constitution was drawn up in French, the language of the ruling elite, and it took a further 70 years for the Flemish to have their tongue acknowledged as Belgium's 'second' language, all of which heightened cultural tensions. The late-19th-century reign of Léopold II brought powerful personal ambition, manifested in the monarch's cruel exploitation of the Congo (p17) and subsequent monumental construction in Brussels, including the Palais des Beaux-Arts and the Parc du Cinquantenaire.

Albert I, who began his rule in 1909, proved to be a much more likable and socially concerned ruler than his tyrannical predecessor. He commanded the Belgian army for most of WWI and practically led the Allied offensive that recaptured the country's coastline in 1918. He survived the battlefield only to die while rock climbing in 1934. In contrast, when Germany invaded Belgium in May 1940, at the start of WWII, Léopold III quickly surrendered to his country's occupiers while his government chose to operate in exile from London. By WWII's end, Belgium's small Jewish population was devastated, its Gypsy minority all but wiped out, and a total of 75,000 of its inhabitants had been killed.

Léopold III abdicated in 1950 due to the furore over his wartime actions, and was replaced by his son, Baudouin. Baudouin granted the Congo independence in 1959 and was popular for his perceived fair treatment of both Walloons and Flemish. However, tensions between the two persisted and in 1962 the regions of Flanders, Wallonia and bilingual Brussels were created, the so-called Linguistic Divide. Baudouin died in 1993; the current king is Albert II.

Brussels became provisional seat of the European Commission in 1958, received NATO in 1967, and is now the headquarters of the economic and political cooperative established in 1993 and called the European Union (EU). Multinationals and foreign agencies have since flooded in and the city's infrastructure has swelled around them, though many locals lament the EU's financial excesses. Public disillusionment with bureaucracy led to the 300,000-strong 1996 'White March' in Brussels, a protest against incompetence during investigations into suspected child murderer Marc Dutroux, who at the time of writing was still awaiting trial. Diverting attention from economic and judicial concerns is Belgium's much-loved royal family, with several marriages and births receiving attention in the new millennium.

The Guilds

In medieval Belgium, traders and craftsmen formed groups known as guilds, setting standards for their craft and establishing local trade monopolies. The guilds, run mainly by wealthy families, also sought to exert political influence over town or city governments to further their own economic interests, particularly in Brussels. During the 16th century, the guilds began building headquarters, initially in wood and then in stone. In Brussels these guildhalls border the old market square, Grand Place, which was the centre of public life at the time – and still is today.

The impressive facade of a guildhall

GOVERNMENT, POLITICS & ECONOMY

Belgium is a constitutional hereditary monarchy, led by King Albert II and a parliament. The parliament consists of the Senate and a Chamber of Representatives, which have responsibility for realms of policy that affect the country as a whole, such as finance, defence and foreign affairs. In one famous example of how a monarch's personal convictions don't always complement parliamentary progress, King Baudouin abdicated for two days in 1990 to avoid giving his approval to a bill legalising abortion – during the 48 hours that he relinquished the throne, the Belgian parliament passed the bill. While this was seen by some Bruxellois as the admirable stance of a principled man, others saw it as a refusal by Baudouin to put the public's desire for change above his own conservative views.

In 1993 the government was decentralised via the signing of the St Michel Accords, which initiated the creation of three regional governments representing the Flemish- and French-speaking communities (Flanders and Wallonia, respectively) and the Brussels-Capital Region. This was another significant step down a long path of constitutional reform that started in the 1960s, when the Flemish, Walloon and German-speaking communities started demanding linguistic, territorial and cultural autonomy. The small German-speaking enclave is based around the towns of Eupen and St Vith in the east of the country, an area given to Belgium as part of German WWII reparations.

Brussels is Belgium's capital and also capital of the Flemish region, while the Ardennes town of Namur is the seat of the Walloon regional government. To add to this governmental complexity, Brussels was also officially designated the capital of Europe in 1993: it's home to the European Commission, the policy-making executive branch of the EU; the publicly elected European Parliament, which keeps an eye on the commission and gives it money; and the Council of Ministers, which ratifies legislation proposed by the commissioners.

The Palais Royal (Royal Palace): open to the public for one month a year (p25)

Belgium's overall political scene has long been dominated by the (Catholic) Christian Democrats, Socialists and Liberals, though support for the green parties (Agalev in Flanders, Ecolo in Wallonia – collectively known as the Greens) is increasing. The right-wing, anti-immigrant and utterly nationalistic Vlaams Blok (Flemish Bloc), which wants full Flemish independence, has gained considerable ground in the past decade. After being governed throughout the 1990s by a seemingly ever-changing coalition headed by Jean-Luc Dehaene from the Christian Democrats, during which time a roll call of political scandals eroded the public's confidence in this party, Belgium opted in 1999 for a rather unusual grouping of Liberals, Socialists and Greens. These parties joined forces to block the progress of the Vlaams Blok and were headed by Guy Verhofstadt, the country's first Liberal prime minister in over 50 years.

EU buildings: serious business

In the 2003 national elections, the Socialists and Liberals won around two-thirds of the available parliamentary seats and renewed their coalition, with Verhofstadt again the leader. The Green party won only a handful of seats, not enough to take a chair at the coalition table. Of most concern, however, was the fact that the Vlaams Blok, campaigning on a platform of 'Our Own People First', won an estimated 20% of the popular vote in Flanders and 10% of the national vote.

Over the centuries, Belgium's economic prosperity has swung from one language community to the other, starting with Flanders' medieval textile wealth, which was later supplanted by Wallonia's coal, iron and steel industries. Then in the 1950s and 1960s, Wallonia's steel and mining industries sank into decline, impoverishing the region, while Flanders became the country's economic powerhouse – the clash between new-found Flemish assertiveness and Wallonian insecurity was the main motivator for the creation of the Linguistic Divide. Today Flanders is still the dominant economic force, but Wallonia is developing high-tech industries such as aeronautics and biotechnology. The country's main industries include financial services, engineering, textiles, machinery and diamonds.

Did You Know?

- population in metropolitan area – 955,000
- average annual wage – US$23,850
- annual inflation rate – 1.7%

The Belgian economy is struggling amid a global economic downturn, a huge public debt (equal to its GDP, which currently stands at US$297.6 billion) and a national unemployment rate of 7%. Brussels accounts for about 15% of the Belgian economy through its industrial, commercial and service activities, including a staggering number of business conferences, and its swelling population has an unemployment rate twice the national average. White-collar workers far outnumber factory workers in the city, due mainly to the 2000-plus foreign companies based here to lobby various EU institutions.

SOCIETY & CULTURE

Read all about it, in French or Flemish

Belgium has a linguistically and culturally divided population of nearly 11 million people, split between Flemish-speaking Flanders (Vlaanderen) in the north with 60% of the population, French-speaking Wallonia (La Wallonie) in the south with 27%, and the German-speaking Eastern Cantons in Belgium's far east, which comprise 13% of the population. The societal mix doesn't stop there, however. Bilingual Brussels is technically in Flanders but dominated by French speakers, and has a multicultural population of nearly one million that includes many other European nationalities, Moroccans, Turks and Africans, the last mainly immigrants from the former Belgian colony of the Congo. The relationship between the large Moroccan community in Schaerbeek and the Bruxellois notably ranges from fearful distrust to cheerful cohabitation. Roughly three-quarters of Belgians are Catholic, with Protestants, Jews and Muslims making up the rest.

The Bruxellois' identity is a curious collage: confident yet modest; sticklers for efficiency, yet with a snail's-pace work ethic that has resulted in a multitude of dramatically overdue building and restoration projects; a love of life and technology, yet a fear of change; and an indigenous sternness, yet a self-effacing and good-humoured cheekiness best embodied in the so-called symbol of the city, Manneken Pis (p25). Belgians resent rules but are simultaneously devoted followers of them – during a visit to the Musées Royaux des Beaux-Arts de Belgique on an afternoon when admission was free to all, we were nonetheless issued a ticket (which read '€0.00') and told to present it for checking at exhibit entrances. The Belgians are also unrelentingly friendly, extremely polite and helpful, and pride themselves on their open intolerance of rudeness and other forms of nastiness. It's worthwhile visiting the dry Musées Bellevue (p23) just to begin to understand the widespread fascination with the Belgian monarchy.

The symbol of Brussels, Manneken Pis

ARTS

Architecture

There's more to Brussels' architecture than the World Heritage–listed Grand Place. The Middle Ages brought ecclesiastical achievements, beginning with Romanesque structures characterised by columns and semicircular arches, and progressing to pointed Gothic arches. The dominant Brabant Gothic style went glam in the 15th century, with a fine example being the beautiful symmetry of the Hôtel de Ville (p25), but it paled against the exuberant ornateness of baroque, a product of the 16th- and early-17th-century Counter-Reformation. Following the 1695 levelling of Grand Place, the guildhalls were rebuilt in a baroque style known as Flemish Renaissance.

Austrian rule in the 18th century bequeathed the city stark but simple neoclassical buildings, on prominent display around Place Royale, followed by a surge of postindependence extravagance that resulted in neo-Renaissance constructions such as the Galeries St Hubert and the gigantic, power-infused creations of Léopold II (look no further than the Palais de Justice; p25). After Art Nouveau, best seen in the work of Victor Horta (p16), came the cool, clean lines of Art Deco, the grandest example being the Musée David et Alice van Buuren (p15). The past 50 years have brought a grab bag of architecture, including the eye-catching Atomium (p24), the ill-fated 'Manhattan' project beside Gare du Nord and the modernistic mayhem of the EU area.

Painting & Sculpture

The vibrant, naturalist works of the 15th-century Flemish primitives were produced by famed artists such as Rogier Van de Weyden, Dirk Bouts, Hans Memling and the man who is widely considered to have invented the oil painting, Jan Van Eyck. Another influential Flemish painter of this era was Hieronymus Bosch, who influenced many later artists with his skilful, often nightmarish visual parables. Arguably the greatest local 16th-century artist was Pieter Breugel the Elder, who painted quirky scenes of

The Talented Mr Magritte

Born in Lessines, north of Mons, René Magritte spent most of his working life in Brussels, where he became one of the world's most prominent surrealist painters. His most famous motif, the man in the bowler hat whose face is hidden from view, exemplified surrealism's rebellion against European rationalism. However, Magritte produced most of his art in a rather conventional house (now the Musée René Magritte; p23) in Jette while wearing a three-piece suit, so his rebellious spirit was ultimately not all that fiery. Some of his famous works are displayed in the Musées Royaux des Beaux-Arts de Belgique (p18).

MARTIN MOOS

contemporary peasant life. Hot on his heels came another Pieter, this one with the surname Rubens, who produced more than 2000 artworks and nurtured baroque artists such as Antoon Van Dyck and Jacob Jordaens.

The 19th century brought the damnable sculptures and canvases of Antoine Wiertz, the famous bronze working-class sculptures of Constantin Meunier, and James Ensor, who graduated from portraiture to more macabre images. Prime 20th-century artists included landscapist Rik Wouters, expressionist Constant Permeke and dreamy surrealists such as René Magritte (see the boxed text on p79) and Paul Delvaux, as well as a strong abstract art movement.

Literature

Belgium's low-key literary career began more or less in the 18th century when Willem Verhoeven and Jan Baptist Verlooy reacted to the French influence in literature with their own individual but Flemish-inspired styles. The following century's writings were imbued with romanticism, which became closely linked with a revival in Flemish nationalist feelings in books such as the historical 1838 novel *De Leeuw van Vlaanderen* (The Lion of Flanders), written by Hendrik Conscience. Flemish poet Guido Gezelle later revived poetry in Flanders with his popular *The Evening and the Rose.*

Popular 20th-century writers include Hugo Claus, who garnered international interest in 1983 with *Het Verdriet van België* (The Sorrow of Belgium), and Marguerite Yourcenar, who became the first woman elected (in 1980) to the male-dominated Académie Française. But arguably the most famous is the prolific Georges Simenon, who wrote serious literature and books about detective Inspector Maigret, and had the year 2003 dedicated to him by European literary circles. Brussels also hosted foreign writers like Charlotte Brontë (see the boxed text on p42) and Victor Hugo who worked on *Les Miserables* here over a 30-year period.

Music

After delving into medieval folk songs, Belgium used carillons (bells attached to town clocks) to great effect and now has a renowned campanology school near Mechelen. Composer André-Modeste Grétry is regarded as the 17th-century father of comic opera, and late-19th-century opera in Brussels was deservedly famous too. But these were topped in the 20th century by Adolphe Sax's invention of the saxophone, jazzy harmonica player Toots Thielemans, Jacques Brel's meteoric rise in French show business, and the delirious 1978 one-hit style of pseudopunk Plastic Bertrand.

Highly successful and modern musos include singer Axelle Red, techno-rockers Praga Khan, the eccentric An Pierlé, the ambient Hooverphonic, the four-piece band Arid and a one-man show called Arno.

Jacques Brel, Brussels' favourite son

Directory

Musée Horta, dedicated to the Art Nouveau stylings of Victor Horta

ARRIVAL & DEPARTURE

Air

The main international touchdown zone is **Brussels International Airport** (Zaventem Airport; 4, C2; www.brusselsairport.be), located 13km northeast of the city centre. The five-storey terminal building has restaurants, bars, a large cafeteria and many other facilities. Level 2 is the arrivals hall, where you'll be greeted by an information desk, a hotel reservations bureau, an ATM, and currency exchange and car-hire counters. Level 3 is the departures hall.

INFORMATION

General enquiries
 info@brusselsairport.be
Flight information
 ☎ 0900 700 00 (within Belgium only)
 ☎ 02 753 77 53 (from abroad)
Car park information
 ☎ 02 753 21 10

AIRPORT ACCESS

From the train station on Level 1, the **Brussels Airport Express** (☎ 02 753 24 40) runs every 20 minutes from 5.30am to 11.45pm to Brussels' three main rail terminals. The trip takes 15 minutes and costs €3.80/2.50 one way (1st/2nd class).

STIB (☎ 02 515 20 00, 0900 103 10; www.stib.irisnet.be – French & Dutch only) runs express bus No 12 from the airport to Schuman metro station and from there to Gare Bruxelles-Luxembourg. The service runs regularly from 5.45am to 10.50pm, taking roughly 30 minutes. Tickets cost €3 and are valid for one hour anywhere on the public transport network. **De Lijn** (☎ 02 526 28 20) runs bus BZ between the airport and Gare du Nord (€2.50, 35 minutes).

A taxi to the Lower Town will cost around €30; use 'official' taxis, which have yellow-and-blue signs.

Bus

Brussels is well connected by long-distance bus to the rest of Europe, including the UK. **Eurolines** (www.eurolines.com), a consortium of coach operators, has a main office (1, E1; ☎ 02 274 13 50; Place Solvay 4, Schaerbeek; 9am-6pm Mon-Fri) beside Gare du Nord, where most buses leave from. A second office (1, B6; ☎ 02 538 20 49; Ave Fonsny 13, St Gilles; 9.30am-5.30pm Mon-Fri, 9.30am-4pm Sat), opposite Gare du Midi, is set in a decrepit-looking building, but the air-conditioned coaches are reasonably comfortable.

Train

National train services are managed by **Belgian Railways** (NMBS/SNCB; ☎ 02 528 28 28; www.b-rail.be), whose logo is a 'B' in an oval. There are four levels of service: InterCity (IC) trains, which are the fastest; InterRegional (IR) trains; local (L) trains; and peak-hour (P) commuter services stopping at specific stations. There's usually an IC or IR train departing every hour or half-hour to each of Belgium's other prime destinations (eg Antwerp, Bruges). All trains have 1st- and 2nd-class carriages with both smoking and nonsmoking sections. Each of Brussels' main stations – **Gare du Nord** (1, E1), **Gare Centrale** (1, D4) and **Gare du Midi** (1, A6) – has an information office.

Gare du Midi is the main station for international travel. **Thalys** (www.thalys.com) operates high-speed trains connecting Brussels to destinations in France (including to Paris in 1½ hours), the Netherlands, Germany and Switzerland; see the website for information and bookings. **Eurostar** (www.eurostar.com) shuttles travellers between Brussels and London's Waterloo station via the Channel Tunnel in two hours, 40 minutes (eight to 10 services daily); the website details the plethora of fares available.

Travel Documents

PASSPORT

Your passport must be valid for another three months beyond your stay – check with your local embassy for the latest information.

VISA

Citizens of the UK, US, Canada, Australia and most European nations, as well as a number of other countries, do not require a visa for stays of up to three months.

Customs & Duty Free

Duty-free goods are no longer sold to those travelling from one EU country to another. For goods purchased in airports or on ferries outside the EU, the usual allowances apply: 200 cigarettes, 50 cigars or 250g of loose tobacco; 1L of spirits plus 2L of wine; 50g of perfume; and other goods to a value of €175.

Left Luggage

The 24-hour lockers at the airport cost between €5 and €7.50, depending on their size. Similar lockers in each of the train stations cost between €2 and €3.25.

GETTING AROUND

Brussels has an extensive, efficient and easy-to-use public transport system, comprising the ultra reliable metro, trams, the premetro (trams that go underground for part of their journey) and buses. Public transport generally runs from 5.30am to 11pm or midnight daily and is managed by the **STIB** (MIVB in Flemish; ☎ 02 515 20 00; www.stib.irisnet.be), with main agencies at Avenue de la Toison d'Or 15 (1, E6), Gare du Midi, and the Rogier and Porte de Namur metro stations. In this book, the nearest metro station is noted after the Ⓜ icon at the end of each listing. Where a premetro station is closer, it's noted after the 🚊 icon.

Remember that to most Belgian drivers, a pedestrian crossing is simply a bit of annoying graffiti – they usually won't stop, even if you've started walking across.

Tickets

Tickets allowing access to all forms of public transport are available from vending machines in metro stations, from STIB kiosks and some newsagents, and on buses and trams. A single-journey ticket is valid for one hour and costs €1.40; five/10-journey tickets cost €6.30/9.20. Day tickets (€3.70) are great value if you'll be jumping on and off public transport all day. You need to validate your ticket at the start of your trip in the machines located at the entrance to metro platforms or inside buses and trams.

Metro

Brussels' metro system has been operating since 1965, with its stations embellished by bars (De Brouckère, Botanique), a chapel (Madou) and nearly 60 works of art (ask the STIB for a brochure). There are three lines: Line 1A (yellow) goes from Roi Baudouin station to Herrmann-Debroux; Line 1B (red) runs from Erasmus to Stockel; and Line 2 (orange) loops around from Simonis to Clémenceau. At the time of writing, Line 2 was being pushed west to link up with Gare de l'Ouest station on Line 1B. Stations are marked by rectangular signs with a white 'M' on a blue background.

Tram, Premetro & Bus

Before negotiating the city's extensive tram and bus network, pick up STIB's free transport map. Premetro trams run mainly underneath the boulevards running between Gare du Nord and Gare du Midi, but also duck down out of sight at other places around town.

Taxi

Taxis are metered, expensive and driven pugnaciously. Taxes and tips are officially included in the meter price. The basic tariff is €2.35, plus €1.14 per kilometre within the Brussels region and €2.28 per kilometre outside it. Between 10pm and 6am, an extra €1.85 is charged per trip. If you need a cab, ring **Taxi Jaune** (☎ 02 569 05 20) or **Taxi Verts** (☎ 02 349 49 49).

Car & Motorcycle

On a short trip to Brussels you're unlikely to need your own wheels, and the take-no-prisoners driving habits do not make motoring a pleasant experience here. However, if you do need to hire a vehicle, you could try **National/Alamo** (☎ 02 753 20 60), **Budget** (☎ 02 753 21 70) or **Europcar** (☎ 02 721 05 92), all with desks at the airport.

PRACTICALITIES

Climate & When to Go

Brussels' mild maritime climate is unfortunately characterised by lots of grey, rainy weather. The warmest months are July and August, though they can also be the wettest – this wasn't the case during the European heat wave of 2003. Weather-wise, the best months to visit are usually April/May and September.

Major events and festivals (see p60) are held throughout the year (except in winter), but the city rarely packs out when these are on. Many arts venues close over summer, so this isn't a good time to visit if your heart's set on theatre or opera. That said, accommodation bargains are plentiful in summer when the Eurocrowd is away on holiday – see the boxed text on p73.

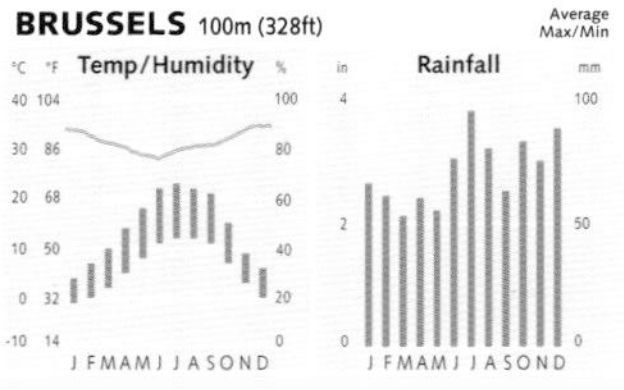

BRUSSELS 100m (328ft)

Average Max/Min

Temp/Humidity — °C °F: 40 104, 30 86, 20 68, 10 50, 0 32, -10 14; %: 100, 80, 60, 40, 20, 0

Rainfall — in: 4, 2, 0; mm: 100, 50, 0

J F M A M J J A S O N D

Disabled Travellers

Belgium is not exactly a world leader when it comes to accessibility for travellers with mobility problems, with many uneven or cobblestoned streets, street-level eateries with stairs at the entrance, few hotels with true barrier-free rooms and centuries' old buildings that require renovation to meet modern standards. Many museums and theatres, however, have wheelchair access, while all train stations have wheelchair ramps. Many metro stations have Braille plaques at the entrance, but the only central station that's accessible by wheelchair is Arts-Loi. Whether travelling by train or visiting a theatre or museum, always give advance notice of the need to accommodate a wheelchair. **Taxi Hendriks** (☎ 02 752 98 00) provides a taxi service for disabled people.

Listings in this book that are wheelchair-friendly are marked by the ♿ icon and rated from 'fair' to 'excellent', with 'fair' meaning a minimal level of accessibility.

Discounts

Many of Brussels' attractions and entertainment venues offer discounts for students and children, though family rates are rare. Students will need to produce an International Student Identity Card (ISIC) in order to qualify for reduced admission to museums and other sights, cinema tickets and train fares. The official 'over 55' cards, which Belgian senior citizens use to obtain concessions, are not available to foreigners, but elderly tourists may find themselves being given a discount anyway; disabled visitors face a similar situation where concessions apply.

The Brussels Card provides free admission to 30 museums and unlimited use of public transport – see p21. For more on museum freebies, see the boxed text on p23.

Electricity

Voltage	220V
Frequency	50Hz
Cycle	AC
Plugs	two round pins, adaptors widely available

Embassies

Australia (1, F4; ☎ 02 286 05 00; www.austemb.be; 5th fl, Rue Guimard 6, Upper Town)
Canada (☎ 02 741 06 11; www.dfait-maeci.gc.ca/canadaeuropa/brussels; Ave Tervuren 2, Etterbeek)
France (1, F4; ☎ 02 548 87 11; www.ambafrance-be.org – French & Dutch only; Rue Ducale 65, Upper Town)
Germany (☎ 02-774 19 11; Ave de Tervuren 190, Etterbeek)
Netherlands (☎ 02 679 17 11; www.nederlandseambassade.be – French & Dutch only; Ave Herrmann-Debroux 48, Auderghem)
New Zealand (1, F5; ☎ 02 512 10 40; 7th fl, Square de Meeûs 1, Upper Town)
UK (3, A1; ☎ 02 287 62 11; www.britishembassy.gov.uk; Rue d'Arlon 85, EU Area)
US (1, F4; ☎ 02 508 21 11; www.usembassy.be; Blvd du Régent 27, Upper Town)

Emergencies

Brussels is a very safe city to walk around, day or night, and the biggest hassle you're likely to face is the unwanted attention of a pickpocket when Grand Place is at its busiest. There are some places, however, where it's better not to wander around in the wee hours, specifically the Gare du Nord area and the industrial district around the Canal de Charleroi west of the centre.

Ambulance	☎ 100
Fire	☎ 100
Police	☎ 101
Police (nonemergency)	☎ 02 279 79 07
Rape Crisis Line	☎ 02 534 36 36

Fitness

The Bruxellois aren't the fittest-looking people around (sports champions like Justine Henin-Hardenne and Kim Clijsters aside), probably due to the proximity of so much quality beer and chocolate. When they can be bothered tearing themselves away from a restaurant table, you'll find them pounding down the gravel trails in the Parc de Bruxelles (1, E4) or hanging out at one of the following places.

John Harris Fitness (2, F3; ☎ 02 219 82 54; www.johnharrisfitness.com; 7th fl, Radisson SAS, Rue Fossé aux Loups 47, Lower Town; 🕒 6.30am-10pm Mon-Fri, 10am-7pm Sat & Sun)
Passage FitnessFirst (1, D1; ☎ 02 274 29 20; www.passagefitness.be – French & Dutch only); Ave de Boulevard 21, St Josse; 🕒 7am-10pm Mon & Tue, 9am-10pm Wed-Fri, 10am-6pm Sat & Sun)
Piscine Victor Boin (☎ 02 539 06 15; Rue de la Perche, St Gilles)

Gay & Lesbian Travellers

Attitudes to homosexuality have become less conservative in Brussels in recent years, evidenced by a burgeoning gay bar/club population around Rue du Marché au Charbon. The local lesbian scene, however, is harder to pin down, with venues regularly opening and closing. The city's premier French-speaking gay and lesbian meeting place is **Tels Quels** (2, B6; ☎ 02 512 32 34; www.telsquels.be – French only; Rue du Marché au Charbon 81), which publishes an eponymous monthly French-language magazine listing bars, restaurants and activities, and also runs an anonymous helpline called **Télégal** (☎ 02 502 00 70; 🕒 8pm-midnight).

Health

IMMUNISATIONS

There are no specific vaccination requirements for Belgium.

PRECAUTIONS

Although Belgium has a poor environmental record, which includes the pumping of sewage straight into the River Senne and extravagant waste production, the standard of living in Brussels is generally quite high, so precautions such as boiling tap water are not necessary.

MEDICAL SERVICES

Belgium has an excellent, extensive health-care system, and most doctors speak English. EU citizens are eligible for free emergency medical care (if they have an E111 certificate), but everyone else should organise medical insurance or be prepared to pay. Hospitals and medical centres with 24-hour accident and emergency departments include **Centre Hospitalier Universitaire Saint-Pierre** (1, C6; ☎ 02 535 40 55 for adults, 02 535 43 60 for children; Rue Haute 322, Marolles) and **Clinique Saint-Jean** (1, E2; ☎ 02 221 91 12; Rue de Marais, Lower Town). You can also contact on-call doctors and pharmacists (day or night) on ☎ 02 479 18 18. For vets on call, ring ☎ 02 479 99 90.

DENTAL SERVICES

If you chip a tooth or require emergency treatment, dial ☎ 02 426 10 26 to contact dentists on call.

PHARMACIES

There are **Multipharma** outlets with long opening hours at Rue du Marché aux Poulets 37 (2, C4; ☎ 02 511 35 90), Place de la Monnaie 10 (2, E3; ☎ 02 217 43 88) and Rue Royale 178 (1, E2; ☎ 02 217 43 73), all in or near the Lower Town. Out-of-hours services are listed in pharmacy windows. The Flemish word for pharmacy is *apotheek*.

Holidays

1 January	New Year's Day
March/April	Easter Monday
1 May	Labour Day
40th day after Easter	Ascension Day
7th Monday after Easter	Whit Monday
21 July	Belgium National Day
15 August	Assumption
1 November	All Saints' Day
11 November	Armistice Day
25 December	Christmas Day

Internet

Brussels is pretty switched on as far as the Internet goes, a fact evidenced by the overwhelming number of Internet Service Providers (ISPs) advertised in the local Yellow Pages. Most upper-end hotels have data ports in each room, and/or business centres that utilise the country's impressive TV cable network to provide super-quick online access.

INTERNET SERVICE PROVIDERS

Belgium's largest ISP is **Skynet** (☎ 02 706 13 11; www.skynet.be – French & Dutch only), which is operated by the national telecommunications giant Belgacom. Other major ISPs with dial-in nodes in Brussels are **AOL** (www.aol.com) and **CompuServe** (www.compu serve.com).

INTERNET CAFÉS

The only sizable Internet café in central Brussels at the time of our research was the huge, charmless **Easyeverything** (2, E2; ☎ 02 211 08 20; Place de Brouckère 9, Lower Town; 9am-midnight). The minimum charge is €0.50 and the average hourly price (depending on demand) is €1.30. You can also do printing on the ground floor.

USEFUL WEBSITES

The Lonely Planet website (www .lonelyplanet.com) offers a speedy link to many of Belgium's websites. Others to try include:

Belgium for Beer Lovers (www.visit belgium.com/beer.htm) All about the amber liquid and where to find it.

City of Brussels' official website (www.bruxelles.irisnet.be) Information on transport, sights and activities, culture, business, the EU and more.

Noctis (www.noctis.com) Entertainment listings for night owls and party animals.

Yellow (Golden) Pages (www.pages dor.be) Worth their weight in gold.

Lost Property

To contact 'lost and found' at Brussels International Airport, dial ☎ 02 753 68 20. If you lose something on the public transport network contact STIB (☎ 02 515 23 94); for losses on the railway call the Belgian Railways (☎ 02 528 28 28).

Metric System

Belgium uses the metric system. Decimals are indicated with commas, thousands with points (full stops). In Flemish shops, 250g is called a *half pond* and 500g a *pond*.

TEMPERATURE

°C = (°F - 32) ÷ 1.8
°F = (°C x 1.8) + 32

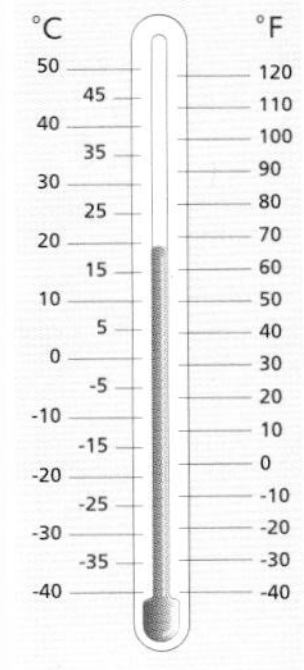

DISTANCE

1in = 2.54cm
1cm = 0.39in
1m = 3.3ft = 1.1yd
1ft = 0.3m
1km = 0.62 miles
1 mile = 1.6km

WEIGHT

1kg = 2.2lb
1lb = 0.45kg
1g = 0.04oz
1oz = 28g

VOLUME

1L = 0.26 US gallons
1 US gallon = 3.8L
1L = 0.22 imperial gallons
1 imperial gallon = 4.55L

Money

CURRENCY

The unit of currency in Belgium is the euro, made up of 100 cents. There are notes of €500, €200, €100, €50, €20, €10 and €5, and coins in denominations of €2, €1 and 50, 20, 10, five, two and one cents.

TRAVELLERS CHEQUES

These are not common currency in Belgium, which prefers cold hard euro cash or the feel of plastic. The office of **American Express** (☎ 02 676 21 21; Blvd du Souverain 100, Watermael-Boitsfort) is well outside the city centre.

CREDIT CARDS

Most credit cards are widely accepted. For cancellations or assistance, call **American Express** (☎ 02 676 21 21), **Diners Club** (☎ 02 206 98 00), **MasterCard** (☎ 0800 150 96) or **Visa** (☎ 0800 183 97).

ATMS
ATMs are becoming more widespread around the city and you won't have too much trouble finding one that can handle Visa, MasterCard, Plus or Cirrus.

CHANGING MONEY
Easy places to change money are banks and foreign-exchange bureaus (*bureaux de change* in French, *wisselkantoren* in Flemish) such as **Camrail Exchange** (1, A6; ☎ 02 556 36 00; Gare du Midi, St Gilles). Banks charge around €1.50 commission on currency transactions, while exchange bureaus usually have better rates but higher fees.

Newspapers & Magazines
There's no shortage of international newspapers and magazines, including many from the UK and US. The widely available English-language magazine the *Bulletin* (€2.50) is published on Thursday and has national news and a decent national entertainment guide.

Opening Hours
Generally, shops are open from 8.30am or 9am until 5.30pm or 6pm Monday to Saturday. Those in and around Grand Place tend to keep longer hours and stay open on Sunday and public holidays. Banks tend to open from 9am to 4pm or 5pm weekdays and Saturday morning, while post offices open from 9am to 5pm or 6pm weekdays and Saturday until noon.

Photography & Video
Film is widely available. High-speed film (200 ASA or higher) is recommended due to the city's relatively dark conditions – skies are often overcast and buildings cast shadows. Local video and TV operate on the PAL system that predominates in Europe and Australia, but isn't compatible with the US NTSC or French SECAM systems.

Post
Belgium's **La Poste** (www.laposte.be) is very efficient and reliable. Brussels' **main post office** (2, D2; ☎ 02 226 39 00; Blvd Anspach, Lower Town) is on the 1st floor of the Centre Monnaie. There's another main branch in St Gilles (Map p33; ☎ 02 539 19 62; Chaussée de Charleroi 31) and an office at the rear of Gare du Midi (1, B6; ☎ 02 524 43 08; Ave Fonsny 48).

POSTAL RATES
There are two rates for sending letters: *prioritaire* (priority) and *non-prioritaire* (nonpriority). Within Belgium, letters weighing less than 50g cost €0.49/0.41 priority/nonpriority; for letters to other European countries it's €0.59/0.52 and to the rest of the world it's €0.84/0.57.

Radio
BBC World Service (648AM) International news and features.
Musique 3 (91.2FM) Classical music.
Radio 21 (93.2FM) Commercial music and electronica.
Radio Wallonie (92.8FM, 101.1FM) A bit of everything.

Telephone
Calls to anywhere within Belgium cost €0.05 per minute during peak time (8am to 7pm Monday to Friday) and €0.03 per minute during off-peak time. Most numbers prefixed with 0900 or 070 are pay-per-minute calls, while those preceded by 0800 are free calls. Phone booths are widespread and take a mixture of coins, phone cards and credit cards. A central **Belgacom sales office** (2, D3; ☎ 02 223 32 29, 0800 338 00; www.belgacom.be) is at Place de la Monnaie 9.

PHONECARDS

A variety of fixed-value and rechargeable phonecards enabling local and international calls are available from Belgacom Téléboutiques, post offices and newsagents.

MOBILE PHONES

Belgium uses GSM 900/1800, compatible with the rest of Europe and Australia, but not with the systems used in North America or Japan. Belgacom outlets can provide phones, SIM cards and accessories. Mobile numbers begin with 0475 to 0479, 0486 or 0496.

COUNTRY & CITY CODES

The country code for Belgium is ☎ 32. Brussels' old area code (02) has been incorporated into local phone numbers.

USEFUL PHONE NUMBERS

Local Directory Inquiries	☎ 1405
International Direct Dial Code	☎ 00
International Directory Inquiries	☎ 1405
International Operator	☎ 1324, 1224
Time	☎ 1300 (in French)

Television

Cable television is huge here (an estimated 95% of the population are hooked up), providing access to international networks such as BBC and CNN, and dozens of other channels. Some of the Flemish-language TV stations regularly broadcast English-language television series and movies.

Time

Belgium runs on Central European Time (GMT/UTC plus one hour). Daylight-savings time is in place from the last Sunday in March to the last Sunday in October.

Tipping

Tipping is not obligatory, as service and value-added tax (VAT) are included in hotel and restaurant prices, but go ahead if you appreciate the service.

Toilets

The charge for using toilets varies between €0.30 and €0.50, payable to the attendant. Aside from in train stations and shopping centres, public toilets are few and far between.

Tourist Information

Tourist Information Brussels (TIB; 2, D5; ☎ 02 513 89 40; www.brusselstourism.com; Hôtel de Ville, Grand Place; ⏲ 9am-6pm) is a cramped but helpful information centre with material specific to Brussels. Around the corner is the combined office of the **Flemish and Walloon tourist authorities** (2, E5; ☎ 02 504 03 90; www.opt.be, www.visitflanders.com; Rue du Marché aux Herbes 63; ⏲ 9am-6pm Mon-Sat, 9am-1pm Sun Nov-Apr; 9am-6pm Mon-Fri, 9am-1pm & 2-6pm Sat & Sun May, Jun, Sep & Oct; 9am-7pm Mon-Fri, 9am-1pm & 2-7pm Sat & Sun Jul & Aug), which has some information on Brussels but concentrates more on national tourism.

Women Travellers

Belgium is a reserved country that's dominated by its own linguistic rift, so women's issues don't feature that prominently here. Regardless, women should encounter few problems in Brussels, and the locals are usually more than willing to assist anyone who's being hassled. Tampons and sanitary pads are widely available in Brussels, and the contraceptive pill is available by prescription.

LANGUAGE

Belgium's Linguistic Divide is most apparent in Brussels, which lies within Flemish-speaking Flanders but whose population mostly speaks French. English is also widely spoken to accommodate visiting businesspeople, politicians and sightseers, but it would be wrong to assume that *everyone* in Brussels speaks English. If you're going to roam beyond the tourist districts a knowledge of useful French words and their Flemish (a form of Dutch) equivalents would be handy. For an guide to French, see Lonely Planet's *French phrasebook*.

BASICS	FRENCH	FLEMISH
Hello.	*Bonjour.*	*Goeiedag/Hallo.*
Good morning.	*Bonjour.*	*Goedemorgen.*
Good evening.	*Bonsoir.*	*Goedenavond.*
Good night.	*Bonne nuit.*	*Goedenacht.*
Goodbye.	*Au revoir.*	*Dag* or *Tot ziens.*
Yes.	*Oui.*	*Ja.*
No.	*Non.*	*Nee.*
Please.	*S'il vous plaît.*	*Alstublieft/Alsjeblieft.* (polite/informal)
Thank you.	*Merci.*	*Dank u/je wel* or *Bedankt.*
You're welcome.	*Je vous en prie.*	*Graag gedaan.*
Excuse me.	*Excusez-moi.*	*Pardon/Excuseer mij.*
Sorry.	*Pardon.*	*Sorry.*

LANGUAGE DIFFICULTIES		
Do you speak English?	*Parlez-vous anglais?*	*Spreekt u/spreek je Engels?* (polite/informal)
I understand.	*Je comprends.*	*Ik begrijp het.*
I don't understand.	*Je ne comprends pas.*	*Ik begrijp het niet.*
Please write it down.	*Est-ce que vous pouvez l'écrire?*	*Schrijf het alstublieft/alsjeblieft op.* (polite/informal)

GETTING AROUND		
Go straight ahead.	*Continuez tout droit.*	*Ga rechtdoor.*
left/right	*gauche/droite*	*links/rechts*
airport	*l'aéroport*	*de luchthaven*
taxi stand	*l'arrêt de taxis*	*de taxistandplaats*
bus stop	*l'arrêt d'autobus*	*de bushalte*
train station	*la gare*	*het (trein)station*
metro station	*la station de métro*	*het metrostation*
tram stop	*l'arrêt de tramway*	*de tramhalte*
Where is...?	*Où est...?*	*Waar is...?*
I'd like to go to...	*Je voudrais aller à...*	*Ik wil graag naar...gaan.*
Does this (bus) go to...	*Est-ce que ce bus va à...?*	*Is dit de bus naar...?*
How much is the fare?	*C'est combien le billet?*	*Hoeveel kost de rit?*
Stop here please.	*Arrêtez ici s'il vous plaît.*	*Stop hier alstublieft.*

EATING & DRINKING		
I'm a vegetarian.	*Je suis végétarien/végétarienne.* (m/f)	*Ik ben vegetariër.*
Do you have an English menu?	*Est-ce que vous avez une carte en anglais?*	*Heeft u een menu in het Engels?*

I'd like the set menu.	*Je prends le menu.*	*Ik neem het dagmenu.*
Please bring the bill.	*Pourrais-je avoir l'addition s'il vous plaît?*	*Mag ik de rekening alstublieft?*

SLEEPING

Do you have any rooms available?	*Est-ce que vous avez des chambres libres?*	*Heeft U kamers vrij?*
How much is it per night?	*Quel est le prix par nuit?*	*Hoeveel is het per nacht?*
Is breakfast included?	*Est-ce que le petit déjeuner est compris?*	*Is het ontbijt inbegrepen?*
Can I see the room?	*Est-ce que je peux voir la chambre?*	*Kan ik de kamer zien?*

SHOPPING

How much is it?	*C'est combien?*	*Hoeveel is het?*
Can I look at it?	*Est-ce que je peux le/la voir?* (m/f)	*Kan ik het zien?*
It's too expensive.	*C'est trop cher pour moi.*	*Het is mij te duur.*
I'm just looking.	*Je regarde.*	*Ik kijk alleen maar.*
Do you accept credit cards?	*Est-ce que vous acceptez des cartes de crédit?*	*Neemt u kredietkaarten aan?*

DAYS & NUMBERS

Monday	*lundi*	*maandag*
Tuesday	*mardi*	*dinsdag*
Wednesday	*mercredi*	*woensdag*
Thursday	*jeudi*	*donderdag*
Friday	*vendredi*	*vrijdag*
Saturday	*samedi*	*zaterdag*
Sunday	*dimanche*	*zondag*

0	*zéro*	*nul*
1	*un*	*een*
2	*deux*	*twee*
3	*trois*	*drie*
4	*quatre*	*vier*
5	*cinq*	*vijf*
6	*six*	*zes*
7	*sept*	*zeven*
8	*huit*	*acht*
9	*neuf*	*negen*
10	*dix*	*tien*
11	*onze*	*elf*
12	*douze*	*twaalf*
13	*treize*	*dertien*
14	*quatorze*	*veertien*
15	*quinze*	*vijftien*
16	*seize*	*zestien*
17	*dix-sept*	*zeventien*
18	*dix-huit*	*achttien*
19	*dix-neuf*	*negentien*
20	*vingt*	*twintig*
30	*trente*	*dertig*
40	*quarante*	*veertig*
50	*cinquante*	*vijftig*
60	*soixante*	*zestig*
70	*soixante-dix*	*zeventig*
80	*quatre-vingt*	*tachtig*
90	*quatre-vingt-dix*	*negentig*
100	*cent*	*honderd*
1000	*mille*	*duizend*
one million	*un million*	*een miljoen*
one billion	*un milliard*	*een miljard*

Bilingual sign in Parc Royal

Index

See also separate indexes for Eating (p94), Sleeping (p94) and Shopping (p94), and the Sights Index with map references (p95).

EATING

SLEEPING

SHOPPING

Sights Index

FEATURES

- Eating
- Entertainment, Drinking, Café
- Highlights
- Shopping
- Sights/Activities
- Sleeping

ROUTES

- Tollway
- Freeway
- Primary Road
- Secondary Road
- Tertiary Road
- Lane
- Under Construction
- One-Way Street
- Unsealed Road
- Mall/Steps
- Tunnel
- Walking Path
- Walking Trail
- Track
- Walking Tour

BOUNDARIES

- State, Provincial
- Regional, Suburb
- Ancient Wall

TRANSPORT

- Airport, Airfield
- Bus Route
- Cable-Car, Funicular
- Cycling, Bicycle Path
- Ferry
- General Transport
- Metro
- Monorail
- Rail
- Taxi Rank
- Trail Head
- Tram

AREAS

- Beach, Desert
- Building
- Land
- Mall
- Other Area
- Park/Cemetary
- Sports
- Urban

HYDROGRAPHY

- River, Creek
- Intermittent River
- Canal
- Swamp
- Water

SYMBOLS

- Bank, ATM
- Buddhist
- Castle, Fortress
- Christian
- Diving, Snorkeling
- Embassy, Consulate
- Hospital, Clinic
- Information
- Internet Access
- Islamic
- Jewish
- Lighthouse
- Lookout
- Monument
- Mountain, Volcano
- National Park
- Parking Area
- Petrol Station
- Picnic Area
- Point of Interest
- Police Station
- Post Office
- Ruin
- Telephone
- Toilets
- Zoo, Bird Sanctuary
- Waterfall